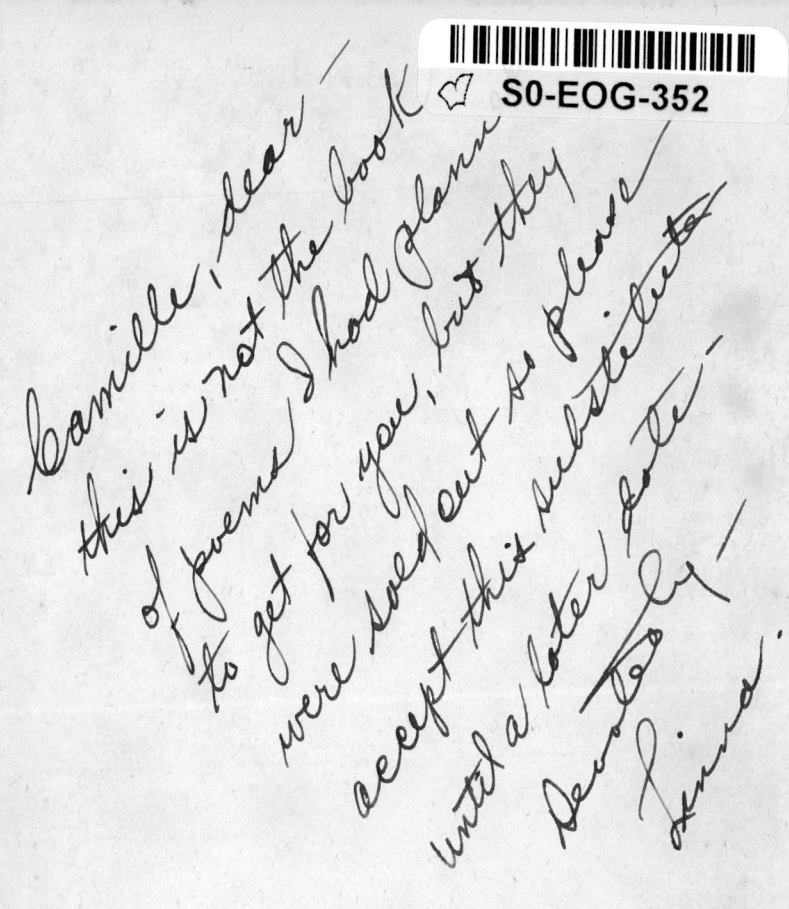

Camille, dear —
this is not the book
of poems I had planned
to get for you, but they
were sold out so please
accept this substitute
until a later date —
Devotedly,
Linna.

A BOOK
OF PERSONAL POEMS

A BOOK OF
PERSONAL POEMS

*Compiled and
Edited by*

WILLIAM R. BOWLIN

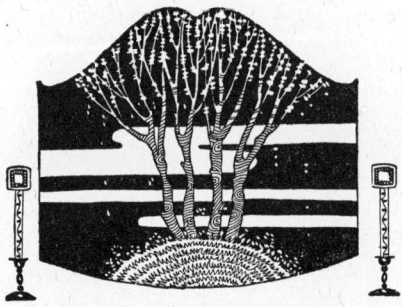

A LAIRD & LEE PUBLICATION
ALBERT WHITMAN
& CO
CHICAGO
1936

COPYRIGHT, 1936, by
ALBERT WHITMAN & CO

ACKNOWLEDGMENTS

Copyright material in this book is used by permission of and special arrangements with: Rose Myra Phillips and Spirit for *Wanderers;* Reverend Philip Jerome Cleveland for *By Night;* Josephine Johnson for *There Is a Tide;* Agnes Lee Freer for *The Christ-Child;* Gerald Raferty and World Call for *Old Teacher;* Douglas Malloch for *As I Grow Old,* and *We Call This Life,* copyright 1927 by Curtis Publishing Company; Lothrop, Lee and Shepard for *Mary Magdalen* and *Black Sheep* by Richard Burton, and *The True Bible* by Sam Walter Foss; William Alexander Percy for *Farmers;* John A. Holmes for *Joshua Peabody* from Younger Poets, permission of Nellie B. Sergent; Mrs. Dorothea Donn-Byrne for *To the World's Edge* by Donn Byrne; Mrs. Elva D. Starbuck for *The Seekers* by Victor Starbuck; Charles Hanson Towne for *Silence,* and *For One Self-Slain;* Alfred A. Knopf for *The Poet* by Witter Bynner; Virginia Eaton for *My Neighbor;* Theodosia Garrison for *Stains, The Days,* and *The Tears of Mary;* Gertie Stewart Phillips and Good Housekeeping for *Prayer;* Judy Van der Veer and Our Dumb Animals for *The Christmas Calf;* Grace Noll Crowell for *Courage to Live;* Thomas Curtis Clark for *Apparitions;* Florence Kiper Frank for *The Jew to Jesus,* and *The Jewish Conscript;* Reverend Clyde McGee for *Mary at the Cross;* Little, Brown and Company for *Revery, Death,* and *The Chariot* by Emily Dickinson; Reverend Robert Freeman for *Beyond the Horizon;* Helen Keller for *In the Garden of the Lord;* Jessie B. Rittenhouse for *Peace* by Clinton Scollard; Edwin Markham for *A Prayer;* The Macmillan Company for *An Old Woman of the Road* by Padraic Colum, and *Let It Be Forgotten,* from Flame and Shadow by Sara Teasdale; Angela Morgan for *Kinship;* Helen Welshimer for *Worship;* Helene Magaret and Atlantic for *Aureole;* Reverend William E. Brooks for *Barabbas;* Margaret E. Sangster and Good Housekeeping for *Campus;* Theresa Lindsey for *The Man, Christ;* Willard Wattles for *A Page from America's Psalter;* William Stanley Braithwaite for *A Song of Living;* and Ethelyn Bryant Chapman for *The Crisis.*

The compiler believes that some poems he has run as *anonymous* are the work of living authors. He also fears that he is doing an injustice in certain other instances where he has been unable to acknowledge authorship. Believing that a great poem is its own excuse for publication, he yet hopes that anyone who knows of poems herein not properly acknowledged will communicate with the publishers that correction may be made in the first subsequent printing.

Printed in U. S. A.

FOREWORD

These poems are for the most part religious, or otherwise concerned with our personal reaction to the conditions and implications of existence. But in no sense are they sectarian, nor expository of any creed save that of faith in God. There are poems generated in the faith of Catholic, Protestant, Jew, and of some not affiliated in any organized religion. Nor is there any division by race, but only the dreams and hopes of men who stand in awe of the Great Cause.

In format, the volume follows closely, but without repetition, the two preceding books of the series—*A Book of Treasured Poems*, and *A Book of Living Poems*. They also contain religious poetry, for a poem that is Treasured, or Living, is generally so because it has struck some deeper chord of our being.

The editor hopes through this volume to bring not only reflection to the thoughtful, but cheer and hope to the ill and discouraged. Having himself for long months studied the blank walls of a hospital room, he feels that a book of personal poems may be very welcome in the lives of many of us.

—*William R. Bowlin*

CONTENTS

	PAGE
Horizon—*Anonymous*	13
Revery—*Emily Dickinson*	13
An Ode—*Joseph Addison*	14
The House of Pain—*Florence Earle Coates*	15
Wanderers—*Rose Myra Phillips*	16
A Well-Bred Man—*William Cowper*	16
To Sleep—*Elizabeth Barrett Browning*	17
The Burial of Moses—*Cecil Frances Alexander*	18
On Seeing a Wounded Hare—*Robert Burns*	19
The High Road—*Anonymous*	20
The Hidden Years at Nazareth—*Allen Eastman Cross*	21
I Heard the Voice of Jesus Say—*Horatius Bonar*	22
Farewell Address at Springfield—*Abraham Lincoln*	23
My Symphony—*William Henry Channing*	24
The Water Mill—*Sarah Doudney*	25
The Heart of the Eternal—*Frederick William Faber*	27
Gone!—*Ethel Runyon Knott*	27
Tomorrows and Tomorrows—*Gertrude Bloede*	28
Wisdom—*The Bible*	28
Oh, May I Join the Choir Invisible—*George Eliot*	29
Immortality—*Joseph Addison*	30
Out to Old Aunt Mary's—*James Whitcomb Riley*	31
By Night—*Philip Jerome Cleveland*	32
A Star—*Anonymous*	33
A Wish—*Samuel Rogers*	34
The Cry of the Children—*Elizabeth Barrett Browning*	35
Onward Christian Soldiers—*Sabine Baring-Gould*	36

	PAGE
My Creed—*Jeanette Gilder*	37
The Bridge—*Henry W. Longfellow*	38
Holy, Holy, Holy!—*Reginald Heber*	40
There Is a Tide—*Josephine Johnson*	41
Rocked in the Cradle of the Deep—*Emma Willard*	42
The Christ-Child—*Agnes Lee*	43
Life—*Samuel Johnson*	43
Charity—*The Bible*	44
So Many—*Frank L. Stanton*	45
A Forest Hymn—*William Cullen Bryant*	46
Old Teacher—*Gerald Raferty*	47
The Rosary—*Robert Cameron Rogers*	47
Snowbound, From—*John Greenleaf Whittier*	48
Boundaries—*Catherine Cate Coblentz*	49
From Sonnet 73—*William Shakspere*	50
Upon the Valley's Lap—*Francis William Bourdillon*	50
As I Grow Old—*Douglas Malloch*	51
The Lost Chord—*Adelaide Proctor*	52
Victory—*Anonymous*	53
A Page from America's Psalter—*Willard Wattles*	54
When God Thought of You—*George MacDonald*	54
The Christ of Common Folks—*George T. Liddell*	55
No Word of Fear—*Walter Savage Landor*	55
Black Sheep—*Richard Burton*	56
My Minde to Me a Kingdom Is—*William Byrd*	57
'Tain't—*Naval Academy Log*	58
Farmers—*William Alexander Percy*	59
Jesus, Saviour, Pilot Me—*Edward Hopper*	60
Joshua Peabody—*John A. Holmes*	61
Mary Magdalen—*Richard Burton*	62
Saved by Grace—*Fanny Crosby*	63
To the World's Edge—*Donn Byrne*	64
Conscience—*William Shakspere*	64
The Ivy Green—*Charles Dickens*	65
The Harvest Waits—*Lloyd Mifflin*	66
Abide With Me—*Henry Francis Lyte*	67

	PAGE
Vesperal—*Silas Weir Mitchell*	68
The Seekers—*Victor Starbuck*	69
For One Who Died—*Jessica Powers*	70
Silence—*Charles Hanson Towne*	70
The Poet—*Witter Bynner*	71
The Anvil—*Anonymous*	72
Lord, Take Away Pain—*Anonymous*	72
My Neighbor—*Virginia Eaton*	73
Stains—*Theodosia Garrison*	74
Prayer—*Gertie Stewart Phillips*	75
We Visit My Estate—*Richard R. Kirk*	75
The Christmas Calf—*Judy Van der Veer*	76
The Ninety and Nine—*Elizabeth C. Clephane*	77
Where Runs the River—*Francis William Bourdillon*	78
The True Bible—*Sam Walter Foss*	79
Our Daily Bread—*Maltbie D. Babcock*	79
I Love to Steal Awhile Away—*Phoebe Brown*	80
O Yet We Trust—*Alfred Tennyson*	81
Good in Everything—*William Shakspere*	81
Indifference—*G. A. Studdert-Kennedy*	82
Why Should We Mourn—*Anonymous*	83
The Good Fight—*William Cullen Bryant*	83
O God, Our Help in Ages Past—*Isaac Watts*	84
Epigram—*Sir William Watson*	85
"My Heart Leaps Up"—*William Wordsworth*	85
The Rustle of a Wing—*Robert G. Ingersoll*	86
Door-Mats—*Mary Caroline Davies*	86
Immanence—*Anonymous*	87
The Days—*Theodosia Garrison*	87
My Faith Looks Up to Thee—*Ray Palmer*	88
Courage to Live—*Grace Noll Crowell*	89
The Jew to Jesus—*Florence Kiper Frank*	90
Apparitions—*Thomas Curtis Clark*	90
The Quiet Life—*Alexander Pope*	91
Circumstance—*Alfred Tennyson*	92
At Jerusalem—*Edna Dean Proctor*	92

	PAGE
With Whom Is No Variableness—*Arthur Hugh Clough*	93
Mary at the Cross—*Clyde McGee*	94
Guidance—*Robert Browning*	94
We Call This Life—*Douglas Malloch*	95
O Love That Lights the Evening Sky—*Louis Fitzgerald Benson*	96
He Lived a Life—*H. N. Fifer*	97
Stricken—*Anonymous*	98
The Primrose Path—*William Shakspere*	98
The Celestial Surgeon—*Robert Louis Stevenson*	99
Still, Still with Thee—*Harriet Beecher Stowe*	99
Hush, My Dear, Lie Still and Slumber—*Isaac Watts*	100
Along the Road—*Robert Brown Hamilton*	101
Joy, Shipmate, Joy—*Walt Whitman*	101
The Old Stoic—*Emily Brontë*	102
From The Universal Prayer—*Alexander Pope*	102
Divina Commedia—*Henry W. Longfellow*	104
The Jewish Conscript—*Florence Kiper Frank*	104
Beyond the Horizon—*Robert Freeman*	105
In the Garden of the Lord—*Helen Keller*	106
Horace	106
God of Our Life Through All the Circling Years—*Hugh T. Kerr*	107
Peace—*Clinton Scollard*	107
A Prayer—*Edwin Markham*	108
O Love That Wilt Not Let Me Go—*George Matheson*	109
The Toys—*Coventry Patmore*	110
To One Self-Slain—*Charles Hanson Towne*	111
An Old Woman of the Road—*Padraic Colum*	112
"Let It Be Forgotten"—*Sara Teasdale*	113
Death—*Emily Dickinson*	113
Evening Hymn—*George Washington Doane*	114
Conscience—*Nathaniel Hawthorne*	114
Life—*Sarojina Nayadu*	115
Kinship—*Angela Morgan*	115
The Tears of Mary—*Theodosia Garrison*	116
Identity—*Thomas Bailey Aldrich*	118
Faith and Hope—*Sir Robert Grant*	119

	PAGE
The Cotter's Saturday Night—*Robert Burns*	120
Aureole—*Helene Magaret*	125
The Difference—*John Bannister Tabb*	125
Providence—*William Cowper*	126
Who Loves the Rain—*Frances Shaw*	127
Stay, Stay at Home, My Heart and Rest—*Henry W. Longfellow*	127
Christ of the Andes—*Florence Earle Coates*	128
He Prayeth Best—*Samuel Taylor Coleridge*	129
Barabbas—*William E. Brooks*	130
Wisdom—*The Bible*	131
Campus—*Margaret Sangster*	132
Come—*Anna Letitia Barbauld*	132
The Mothers of Men—*Joaquin Miller*	133
The Man, Christ—*Theresa Lindsey*	134
My Own Song—*Harriet Prescott Spofford*	135
The Last Word—*Matthew Arnold*	136
Speak Gently—*David Bates*	136
A Song of Living—*William Stanley Braithwaite*	137
The Pledge of Cheerfulness—*William Cowper*	138
Art Thou Weary?—*John Mason Neale*	139
The Ways of Death—*William Ernest Henley*	140
The Crisis—*Ethelyn Bryant Chapman*	141
The Old Amati—*Oliver Wendell Holmes*	142
God Makes a Path—*Roger Williams*	143
The Old Man's Motto—*John Godfrey Saxe*	144
Hudibras—*Samuel Butler*	145
God Chose a Star—*Anonymous*	146
God Rest Ye, Merry Gentlemen—*Dinah Maria Mulock Craik*	146
Guide Me, O Thou Great Jehovah—*William Williams*	147
Thou Art God—*The Bible*	148

A BOOK OF PERSONAL POEMS

A little aid,
Just here and there,
Removes from life
Much toil and care.

HORIZON

Anonymous

And Shakespeare, polishing a new-made rhyme
Lays by his quill to watch old argosies
Flash past the golden headlands of Orion,
Their sails a-flutter in the winds of time.
  —*Victor Starbuck.*

I watched a sail until it dropped from sight
Over the rounding sea. A gleam of white,
A last far-flashed farewell, and, like a thought
Slipt out of mind, it vanished and was not.

Yet to the helmsman standing at the wheel
Broad seas still stretched beneath the gliding keel.
Disaster? Change? He felt no slightest sign,
Nor dreamed he of that far horizon line.

So may it be, perchance, when down the tide
Our dear ones vanish. Peacefully they glide
On level seas, nor mark the unknown bound:
We call it death—to them 'tis life beyond.

 ## REVERY

Emily Dickinson
1830-1886

Sit in revery, and watch the changing color of the waves that break upon the idle seashore of the mind.—Longfellow.

To make a prairie it takes a clover and one bee—
And revery.
The revery alone will do
If bees are few.

[13]

AN ODE

Joseph Addison
1672-1719

*"God sends his teachers unto every age,"
says Lowell. Joseph Addison was such. Following the excesses of the Restoration, Addison attained a leadership over his time that was of immeasurable value to England and to us. Of his burial at midnight in Westminster, the poet Thomas Tikell wrote:*

*Can I forget the dismal night that gave
My soul's best part for ever to the grave?
How silent did his old companions tread,
By midnight lamps, the mansions of the dead. . . .
What awe did the slow solemn knell inspire;
The pealing organ, and the pausing choir;
The duties by the lawn-robed prelate paid:
And the last words, that dust to dust conveyed!*

The spacious firmament on high,
With all the blue ethereal sky,
And spangled heavens, a shining frame,
Their great Original proclaim.
The unwearied sun from day to day
Does his Creator's power display,
And publishes to every land
The work of an almighty Hand.

Soon as the evening shades prevail,
The moon takes up the wondrous tale,
And nightly, to the listening earth,
Repeats the story of her birth;
Whilst all the stars that round her burn,
And all the planets in their turn,
Confirm the tidings as they roll,
And spread the truth from pole to pole.

What though in solemn silence all
Move round the dark terrestrial ball?

What though nor real voice nor sound
Amid their radiant orbs be found?
In reason's ear they all rejoice,
And utter forth a glorious voice,
For ever singing as they shine,
"The Hand that made us is divine!"

THE HOUSE OF PAIN
Florence Earle Coates
1850-1927

And God shall wipe away all tears from their eyes;
And there shall be no more death,
  Neither sorrow nor crying,
Neither shall there be any more pain,
For the former things
  Are passed away.
              —*Revelations 21, 4.*

Unto the Prison House of Pain none willingly repair—
   The bravest who an entrance gain
Reluctant linger there:—
For Pleasure, passing by that door, stays not to cheer the sight,
And Sympathy but muffles sound and banishes the light.

Yet in the Prison House of Pain things full of beauty blow—
   Like Christmas roses, which attain
Perfection 'mid the snow—
Love entering, in his mild warmth the darkest shadows melt,
And often, where the hush is deep, the waft of wings is felt.

Ah, me! the Prison House of Pain!—what lessons there are bought!
   Lessons of a sublimer strain
Than any elsewhere taught;
Amid its loneliness and gloom, grave meanings grow more clear,
For to no earthly dwelling-place seems God so strangely near!

WANDERERS
Rose Myra Phillips

At evening, home is the best place for man.—Goethe.

Heavens are more vast at evening tide
    When swallows' fragile wings,
Veering homeward, seek familiar nests
    From journeyings.

Earth and sky's gold bridal ring still shines
    Within the gloaming west,
Now the same old urge takes hold of me
    For love and rest.

Strange how chimneys pinnacle themselves
    Against the sky at night,
Making wanderers the more aware
    Of homeless plight.

A WELL-BRED MAN
William Cowper
1731-1800

Aaron Burr fought and killed Alexander Hamilton in 1804.

Am I to set my life upon a throw
Because a bear is rude and surly?—No!
A moral, sensible, and well-bred man
Will not affront me, and no other can.

TO SLEEP

Elizabeth Barrett Browning

1806-1861

It is vain for you to rise up early, to sit up late, to eat the bread of sorrows: for so he giveth his beloved sleep.—Psalm 127, 2.

Of all the thoughts of God that are
Borne inward unto souls afar,
Along the Psalmist's music deep,
Now tell me if that any is,
For gift or grace, surpassing this—
  "He giveth His beloved, sleep"?

* * * * *

"Sleep soft, beloved!" we sometimes say,
But have no tune to charm away
Sad dreams that through the eyelids creep:
But never doleful dream again
Shall break the happy slumber, when
  "He giveth His beloved, sleep."

O earth so full of dreary noises!
O men, with wailing in your voices!
O delvèd gold, the wailers heap!
O strife, O curse, that o'er it fall!
God makes a silence through you all,
  And "giveth His beloved, sleep."

* * * * *

And friends, dear friends, when it shall be
That this low breath is gone from me,
And round my bier ye come to weep,
Let one, most loving of you all,
Say, "Not a tear must o'er her fall!
  "He giveth His beloved, sleep."

THE BURIAL OF MOSES

Mrs. Cecil Frances Alexander

1818-1895

And He buried him in a valley in the land of Moab, over against Beth-peor. But no man knoweth of his sepulchre unto this day.
—*Deut. XXXIV, 6.*

By Nebo's lonely mountain, on this side Jordan's wave,
In a vale in the land of Moab, there lies a lonely grave;
But no man dug that sepulchre, and no man saw it e'er,
For the angels of God upturned the sod, and laid the dead man there.

That was the grandest funeral that ever passed on earth;
But no man heard the tramping, or saw the train go forth;
Noiselessly as the daylight comes when the night is done,
And the crimson streak on the ocean's cheek grows into the great sun,—

Noiselessly as the spring-time her crown of verdure weaves,
And all the trees on all the hills open their thousand leaves,—
So, without sound of music, or voice of them that wept,
Silently down from the mountain's crown the great procession swept.

Lo! when the warrior dieth, his comrades of the war,
With arms reversed, and muffled drums, follow the funeral car.
They show the banners taken, they tell his battles won,
And after him lead his masterless steed, while peals the minute-gun.

Amid the noblest of the land men lay the sage to rest,
And give the bard an honored place with costly marble dressed,

In the great minster transept, where lights like glories fall,
And the sweet choir sings, and the organ rings, along the emblazoned wall.

This was the bravest warrior that ever buckled sword;
This the most gifted poet that ever breathed a word;
And never earth's philosopher traced, with his golden pen,
On the deathless page, truths half so sage, as he wrote down for men.

And had he not high honor, the hillside for a pall;
To lie in state while angels wait with stars for tapers tall;
And the dark rock pines, like tossing plumes, over his bier to wave;
And God's own hand, in that lonely land, to lay him in the grave?

O lonely tomb in Moab's land! O dark Beth-peor's hill,
Speak to these curious hearts of ours, and teach them to be still:
God hath his mysteries of Grace—ways that we cannot tell;
He hides them deep, like the secret sleep of him he loved so well.

ON SEEING A WOUNDED HARE

Robert Burns

1759-1796

Burns himself writes: "One morning lately, as I was out pretty early in the fields sowing some grass seeds, I heard the burst of an echo from a neighboring plantation and presently a poor little wounded hare came crippling by me."

The hunter, James Thompson, afterwards said, "He cursed me and said he would not mind throwing me into the water."

    Inhuman man! curse on thy barb'rous art,
      And blasted be thy murder-aiming eye;
      May never pity soothe thee with a sigh,
    Nor ever pleasure glad thy cruel heart!

Go, live, poor wanderer of the wood and field,
  The bitter little that of life remains;
  No more the thickening brakes and verdant plains
To thee shall home, or food, or pastime yield.

Seek, mangled wretch, some place of wonted rest,
  No more of rest, but now thy dying bed!
  The sheltering rushes whistling o'er thy head
The cold earth with thy bloody bosom prest.

Oft as by winding Nith I, musing, wait
  The sober eve, or hail the cheerful dawn,
  I'll miss thee sporting o'er the dewy lawn,
And curse the ruffian's aim, and mourn thy hapless fate.

THE HIGH ROAD

Anonymous

A beautiful fragment.

Wheresoever you may walk
In that far land,—
Whatever company
May share with you the light—
If you can think of friends and things
You used to know,—
You're thinking tenderly of us
Tonight.

But if, perchance, it's
Differently arranged—
If you may not for sadness
Recall the past,—
We'll keep on being lonely
For awhile,
Knowing we'll walk the same high road
At last.

THE HIDDEN YEARS AT NAZARETH

Allen Eastman Cross

1864-

Dr. Cross says of the origin of this poem: "When I was in Palestine, the most challenging places to my imagination were not the monumental shrines of tourist debate, but the open hills and waters of Galilee, and most of all, the little green cup of Nazareth, high up in those hills, . . . I wandered through the old streets and up the hill above the town and found anemonies looking out from among the rocks, as the Boy Jesus must have seen them."

The hidden years at Nazareth!
   How deep and still they seem,
Like rivers flowing in the dark,
   Or waters in a dream!
Like waters under Syrian stars
   Reflecting lights above,
Reflecting in their silent depths
   The wonders of God's love.

The hidden years at Nazareth
   How clear and true they lie,
As open to the smile of God
   As to the Syrian sky!
As open to the heart of man
   As to the genial sun,
With dreams of vast adventuring,
   And deeds of kindness done!

The hidden years at Nazareth
   How radiant they rise,
With life and death in balance laid
   Before a Lad's clear eyes!
O Soul of youth, forever choose
   Forgetting faith or fear,
To live for truth, or die with God
   Who stands beside thee here.

I HEARD THE VOICE OF JESUS SAY

Horatius Bonar
1808-1889

Horatius Bonar was born in Edinburgh and did his work in Scotland. More than one hundred of his hymns are in use today after almost a century. During most of his life he would not allow them to be sung in his own service. It is said that once in later years when he introduced one of them into the morning service, two of his Scotch elders rose and walked stiffly out of the kirk.

I heard the voice of Jesus say,
 "Come unto me and rest;
Lay down, thou weary one, lay down
 Thy head upon my breast!"
I came to Jesus as I was,
 Weary, and worn, and sad;
I found in him a resting-place,
 And he hath made me glad.

I heard the voice of Jesus say,
 "Behold, I freely give
The living water; thirsty one,
 Stoop down, and drink, and live!"
I came to Jesus, and I drank
 Of that life-giving stream;
My thirst was quenched, my soul revived,
 And now I live in him.

I heard the voice of Jesus say,
 "I am this dark world's light;
Look unto me, thy morn shall rise,
 And all thy day be bright!"
I looked to Jesus, and I found
 In him my Star, my Sun;
And in that light of life I'll walk
 Till all my journey's done.

FAREWELL ADDRESS AT SPRINGFIELD

Abraham Lincoln
1809-1865

Under emotion, Lincoln not infrequently spoke in unconscious poetry, of natural, balanced phrases.

On a stormy morning, February 11, 1861, Lincoln went to the little railroad depot in Springfield where a train awaited to take him to Washington and the Presidency of the United States. His neighbors crowded about the waiting room door for a chance to shake his hand and murmur farewells. Some merely pressed his hand and turned away. Says Nicolay and Hay:

"The crowd closed about the railroad car into which the President-elect and his party made their way. . . . The bell gave notice of starting; but as the conductor paused with his hand upon the bell-rope, Mr. Lincoln appeared upon the platform of the car, and raised his hand to command attention. The bystanders bared their heads in the falling snow-flakes, and standing thus, his neighbors heard his voice for the last time in the city of his home, in a farewell address so chaste and pathetic, that it reads as if he already felt the tragic shadow of forecasting fate."

My Friends:
No one, not in my situation,
Can appreciate my feeling of sadness
At this parting.

To this place,
And the kindness of these people,
I owe everything.
Here I have lived a quarter of a century,
And have passed from a young to an old man.
Here my children have been born,
And one is buried.

I now leave
Not knowing when or whether ever I may return,
With a task before me greater than that
Which rested upon Washington.

Without the assistance of that Divine Being
Who ever attended him,
I cannot succeed.
With that assistance,
I cannot fail.

Trusting in Him who can go with me,
And remain with you,
And be everywhere for good,
Let us confidently hope that all will yet be well.

To His care commending you,
As I hope in your prayers you will commend me,
I bid you an affectionate
Farewell.

MY SYMPHONY
William Henry Channing
1810-1884

The popularity and modernness of Channing's My Symphony leads one somehow to think of it as contemporaneous with the reader rather than with Henry Clay. William Henry Channing was a nephew of the great William Ellery Channing, founder of the American Unitarian Association, and was himself a minister of the church.

To live content with small means.
To seek elegance rather than luxury, and refinement rather than fashion.
To be worthy, not respectable, and wealthy, not rich.
To study hard, think quietly, talk gently, act frankly.
To listen to stars and birds, to babes and sages, with open heart.
To bear all cheerfully, do all bravely, await occasion, hurry never.
In a word, to let the spiritual, unbidden and unconscious, grow up through the common.
This is to be my symphony.

THE WATER MILL
Sarah Doudney
1843-

Sarah Doudney was a native of Portsmouth, England. Almost her sole claim to literary fame is this much-quoted poem, which in spite of its mid-Victorian preaching, promises to hold the great popularity it gained among our grandfathers.

Listen to the water mill,
Through the live-long day,
How the clanking of its wheel
Wears the hours away!
Languidly the autumn wind
Stirs the forest leaves
From the field the reapers sing,
Binding up their sheaves;
And a proverb haunts my mind,
As a spell is cast:
"The mill cannot grind
With the water that is past."

Autumn winds revive no more
Leaves that once are shed,
And the sickle cannot reap,
Corn once gatherèd;
Flows the ruffled streamlet on,
Tranquil, deep, and still,
Never gliding back again
To the water mill;
Truly speaks the proverb old,
With a meaning vast,—
"The mill cannot grind
With the water that is past."

Take the lesson to thyself
True and loving heart;
Golden youth is fleeting by,
Summer hours depart;
Learn to make the most of life,
Lose no happy day;
Time will never bring thee back
Chances swept away!
Leave no tender word unsaid,
Love while love shall last;
"The mill cannot grind
With the water that is past."

Work while yet the daylight shines,
Man of strength and will!
Never does the streamlet glide
Useless by the mill;
Wait not till tomorrow's sun
Beams upon the way,
All that thou canst call thine own
Lies in thy "today."
Power and intellect and health
May not always last,
"The mill cannot grind
With the water that is past."

O the wasted hours of life
That have drifted by!
O the good that might have been,—
Lost, without a sigh!
Love, that we might once have saved
By a single word,
Thoughts conceived but never penned,
Perishing unheard;—
Take the proverb to thine heart,
Take, and hold it fast,—
"The mill cannot grind
With the water that is past."

THE HEART OF THE ETERNAL
Frederick William Faber
1814-1863

Like Cardinal Newman, whom he deeply admired, Frederick William Faber began service in the English Church and in later years turned to the Roman Catholic faith. He was a voluminous writer of poetry and prose, and many of his songs are in our church hymnals.

There's a wideness in God's mercy,
Like the wideness of the sea;
There's a kindness in His justice,
Which is more than liberty.

For the love of God is broader
Than the measures of man's mind;
And the heart of the Eternal
Is most wonderfully kind.

If our love were but more simple,
We should take Him at His word,
And our lives would be all sunshine
In the sweetness of our Lord.

GONE!
Ethel Runyon Knott

*And every little while I look,—
But you have gone to stay.*

The shadows miss you, as they gather round your chair;
The breezes long to fluff your silver hair;
The house still stands, the home is forever dead,—
A tired gray shell from which the soul has fled.

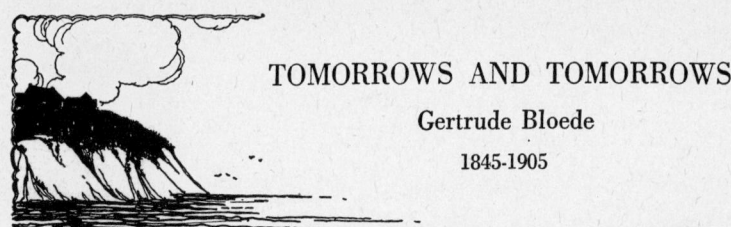

TOMORROWS AND TOMORROWS
Gertrude Bloede
1845-1905

All I have seen teaches me to trust the Creator for all I have not seen.
—Emerson.

Tomorrows and tomorrows stretch a gray
   Unbroken line of shore; but as the sea
Will fret and gnaw the land, and stealthily
Devour it grain by grain, so day by day
Time's restless waters lap the sands away,
   Until the shrinking isle of life, where we
   Had pitched our tent, wholly engulfed shall be,
   And swept far out into eternity,
Some morn, some noon, some night—we may not say
   Just how, or when, or where; and then—what then?
   O cry unanswered still by mortal ken!

This only may we know,—how far and wide
That precious dust be carried by the tide,
No mote is lost, but every grain of sand
Close-gathered in our Father's loving hand,
And made to build again—somehow, somewhere—
Another Isle of Life, divinely fair!

WISDOM
The Bible
From Proverbs, 16, 17, and 18.

Length of days is in her right hand;
And in her left hand riches and honor.
Her ways are ways of pleasantness,
And all her paths are peace.
She is a tree of life to them
That lay hold upon her:
And happy is every one
That retaineth her.

[28]

OH, MAY I JOIN
THE CHOIR INVISIBLE
George Eliot

1819-1880

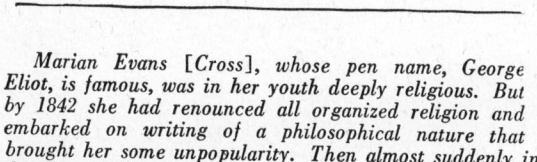

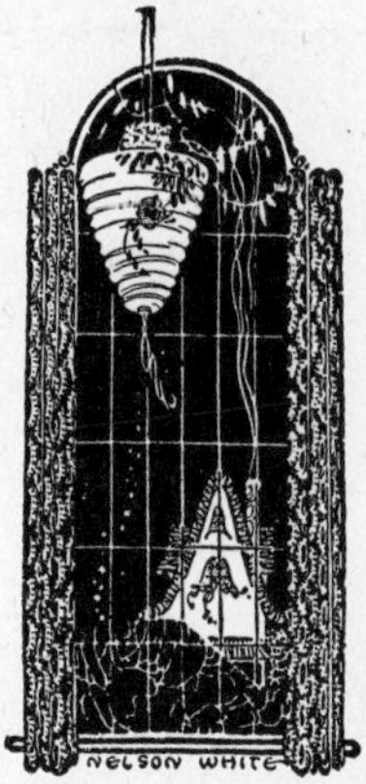

Marian Evans [Cross], whose pen name, George Eliot, is famous, was in her youth deeply religious. But by 1842 she had renounced all organized religion and embarked on writing of a philosophical nature that brought her some unpopularity. Then almost suddenly in 1867 came the poem Oh, May I Join the Choir Invisible, which instantly became famous and for a generation was almost a lay Bible among churches.

    Oh, may I join the choir invisible
    Of those immortal dead who live again
    In minds made better by their presence: live
    In pulses stirred to generosity,
    In deeds of daring rectitude, in scorn
    For miserable aims that end with self,
    In thoughts sublime that pierce the night like stars,
    And with their mild persistence urge man's search
    To vaster issues.
               So to live is heaven:
    To make undying music in the world,
    Breathing as beauteous order that controls
    With growing sway the growing life of man.
    So we inherit that sweet purity
    For which we struggled, failed, and agonized,
    With widening retrospect that bred despair.
    Rebellious flesh that would not be subdued,
    A vicious parent shaming still its child,
    Poor anxious penitence, is quick dissolved;
    Its discords, quenched by meeting harmonies,
    Die in the large and charitable air.
    And all our rarer, better, truer self,
    That sobbed religiously in yearning song,

That watched to ease the burden of the world,
Laboriously tracing what must be,
And what may yet be better,—saw within
A worthier image for the sanctuary,
And shaped it forth before the multitude,
Divinely human, raising worship so
To higher reverence more mixed with love,—
That better self shall live till human Time
Shall fold its eyelids, and the human sky
Be gathered like a scroll within the tomb,
Unread forever.
              This is life to come,
Which martyred men have made more glorious
For us, who strive to follow.
                         May I reach
That purest heaven, be to other souls
The cup of strength in some great agony,
Enkindle generous ardor, feed pure love,
Beget the smiles that have no cruelty,
Be the sweet presence of a good diffused,
And in diffusion ever more intense.
So shall I join the choir invisible
Whose music is the gladness of the world.

 ## IMMORTALITY

Joseph Addison
1672-1719

Plato, Greek philosopher of 400 B. C., postulated immortality by the argument that all our concepts are re-cognitions—that is, echoes of a previous existence: hence a succeeding state of being.

It must be so, Plato, thou reasonest well!—
Else whence this pleasing hope, this fond desire,
This longing after immortality:
Or whence this secret dread, and inward horror
Of falling into naught? Why shrinks the soul
Back on herself, and startles at destruction?
'Tis the divinity that stirs within us,
'Tis heaven itself that points out an hereafter,
And intimates eternity to man.

OUT TO OLD AUNT MARY'S*

James Whitcomb Riley

1849-1916

James Whitcomb Riley, beloved "Poet Laureate of Indiana," used this poem as the title-piece of a volume of poems published in 1904. It deserves its long popularity. However the styles of verse may change, poems of the Old Aunt Mary type will live, for of such is the kingdom of poetry.

Wasn't it pleasant, O brother mine,
In those old days of the lost sunshine
Of youth—when the Saturday's chores were through,
And the "Sunday's wood" in the kitchen, too,
And we went visiting, "me and you,"
    Out to Old Aunt Mary's?

It all comes back so clear today!
Though I am as bald as you are gray—
Out by the barn-lot, and down the lane,
We patter along in the dust again,
As light as the tips of the drops of the rain,
    Out to Old Aunt Mary's!

We cross the pasture, and through the wood
Where the old gray snag of the poplar stood,
Where the hammering "red-heads" hopped awry,
And the buzzard "raised" in the "clearing" sky
And lolled and circled, as we went by
    Out to Old Aunt Mary's.

*From *Afterwhiles*, by James Whitcomb Riley. Copyright 1887, 1915. Used by special permission of the Publishers, The Bobbs-Merrill Company.

And then in the dust of the road again;
And the teams we met, and the countrymen;
And the long highway, with sunshine spread
As thick as butter on country bread,
Our cares behind, and our hearts ahead
    Out to Old Aunt Mary's.

Why, I see her now in the open door,
Where the little gourds grew up the sides and o'er
The clapboard roof!—And her face—ah, me!
Wasn't it good for a boy to see—
And wasn't it good for a boy to be
    Out to Old Aunt Mary's?

And O my brother, so far away,
This is to tell you she waits today
To welcome us:—Aunt Mary fell
Asleep this morning, whispering, "Tell
The boys to come!" And all is well
    Out to Old Aunt Mary's.

BY NIGHT
Philip Jerome Cleveland

A beautiful thought done beautifully. Mr. Cleveland is a Congregational minister in New England.

The tapers in the great God's hall
Burn ageless, beautiful and white;
But only with the fall of dusk.
Disclose to earth their faithful light.

Earth keeps her lamps of beauty, too,
Fairer than stars in fields above.
Dark hours of grief and pain reveal
The undreamed constancy of love.

A STAR
Anonymous

*O freshening star above the old
Worn hills of Bethlehem.*

A star has stopped above my heart—
I am aware
Of silver dust upon my face,
And through my hair.
I feel the star points lengthening
Along the air.

A star has stopped above my heart—
So blinding, white—
I cannot see, I cannot breathe,
It is so bright!
It blooms, this silver annual,
Each Christmas night.

A star has stopped above my heart,
A flower in flame.
The same star that stood over Him
The night He came.
I turn, the quick tears in my eyes,
And call His Name.

A WISH
Samuel Rogers
1763-1855

During a long life Samuel Rogers was the connecting link between two great literary periods—that of Johnson and Goldsmith, and the period of Tennyson and Swinburne. He was the friend of Byron and, though he greatly admired Burns, to his great disappointment he missed him on a tour to Scotland in 1787. He refused the Laureateship in 1850. In its honest simplicity, A Wish resembles the best of our modern poetry.

Mine be a cot beside the hill;
A bee-hive's hum shall soothe my ear;
A willowy brook that turns a mill,
With many a fall shall linger near.

The swallow, oft, beneath my thatch
Shall twitter from her clay-built nest;
Oft shall the pilgrim lift the latch,
And share my meal, a welcome guest.

Around my ivied porch shall spring
Each fragrant flower that drinks the dew;
And Lucy, at her wheel, shall sing
In russet-gown and apron blue.

The village-church among the trees,
Where first our marriage vows were given,
With merry peals shall swell the breeze
And point the taper spire to Heaven.

THE CRY OF THE CHILDREN

Elizabeth Barrett Browning

1806-1861

*In the England of 1850, industrial cruelty was at its height. Says Cheney—
"In Christian England, it was unendurable that women and little children
should work longer hours, be condemned to greater hardships, and be more
completely cut off from the enjoyments of life than were the slaves of tropical
countries." Mrs. Browning's poem was a powerful influence for reform.*

"Do ye hear the children weeping, O my brothers,
    Ere the sorrow comes with years?
They are leaning their young heads against their mothers,
    And that cannot stop their tears.
The young lambs are bleating in the meadows;
    The young birds are chirping in the nest;
The young fawns are playing with the shadows;
    The young flowers are blowing toward the west;
But the young, young children, O my brothers!
    They are weeping bitterly.
They are weeping in the play-time of the others
    In the country of the free.

    *   *   *   *   *

'For oh!' say the children, 'we are weary,
    And we cannot run or leap:
If we cared for any meadows, it were merely
    To drop down in them and sleep.'

    *   *   *   *   *

"They look up with their pale and sunken faces,
    And their looks are dread to see,
For they mind you of their angels in high places,
    With eyes turned to Deity.
'How long,' they say, 'how long, O cruel nation,
    Will you stand, to move the world on a child's heart,
Stifle down with a mailed heel its palpitation
    And tread onward to your throne amid the mart?' "

ONWARD CHRISTIAN SOLDIERS
Sabine Baring-Gould
1834-1924

The famous marching hymn of the Masonic fraternity, Onward Christian Soldiers, was written by the Reverend Sabine Baring-Gould, a Church of England rector at Harbury, England, one beautiful night in 1865. There was to be next day a union of his and a church in a neighboring village, and he desired a fitting march song for the children of his congregation on their way through country lane and meadow to join their friends at Whitmonday festival. The first tune, however, was not the grand marching paean that we know. The present music was written in 1871 by Sir Arthur Sullivan, composer of the Gilbert and Sullivan light operas, and of the music of The Lost Chord.
Sabine Baring-Gould wrote also Now the Day Is Over.

Onward, Christian soldiers,
　Marching as to war,
With the cross of Jesus
　Going on before.
Christ the royal master
　Leads against the foe;
Forward into battle,
　See his banners go.

At the sound of triumph
　Satan's host doth flee;
On, then, Christian soldiers,
　On to victory!
Hell's foundations quiver
　At the shout of praise;
Brothers lift your voices,
　Loud our anthems raise.

Like a mighty army
　Moves the church of God;
Brethren, we are treading
　Where the saints have trod;

We are not divided,
   All one body, we,
One in hope and doctrine,
   One in charity.

Crowns and thrones may perish,
   Kingdoms rise and wane,
But the church of Jesus
   Constant will remain;
Gates of hell can never
   'Gainst that church prevail;
We have Christ's own promise
   And that cannot fail.

Onward, then, ye people!
   Join our happy throng,
Blend with ours your voices,
   In the triumph song;
Glory laud and honor
   Unto Christ the king;
This through countless ages
   Men and angels sing.

MY CREED

Jeanette Gilder

1849-1916

Jeanette Gilder and her famous brother Richard Watson Gilder have now both passed the Gates.

I do not fear to tread the path that those I love long since have trod;
I do not fear to pass the gates and stand before the living God.
In this world's fight I've done my part; if God be God He knows it well;
He will not turn His back on me and send me down to blackest hell
Because I have not prayed aloud and shouted in the market place.
'Tis what we do, not what we say, that makes us worthy of His grace.

THE BRIDGE

Henry W. Longfellow

1807-1882

The Bridge has been criticised for its sentimentality and its built-up emotionalism, and parodied by those who have a pleasure in marring things. But sentiment, especially sorrow, is a reality. The death in 1835 by accident, of his wife, left Longfellow permanently saddened. "Hardly a day passes," he wrote, "that some face or familiar object, or some passage from the book I am reading, does not call up the image of my beloved wife so vividly that I pause and burst into tears—and sometimes cannot rally again for hours."

Years are great physicians

> *But now it has fallen from me*
> *It is buried in the sea.*

I stood on the bridge at midnight,
  As the clocks were striking the hour,
And the moon rose o'er the city,
  Behind the dark church-tower.

I saw her bright reflection
  In the waters under me,
Like a golden goblet falling
  And sinking into the sea.

And far in the hazy distance
  Of that lovely night in June,
The blaze of the flaming furnace
  Gleamed redder than the moon.

Among the long, black rafters
  The wavering shadows lay,
And the current that came from the ocean
  Seemed to lift and bear them away,

As, sweeping and eddying through them,
  Rose the belated tide,
And, streaming into the moonlight,
  The seaweed floated wide.

And like those waters rushing
  Among the wooden piers,
A flood of thoughts came o'er me
  That filled my eyes with tears.

How often, oh, how often,
  In the days that had gone by,
I had stood on that bridge at midnight
  And gazed on that wave and sky!

How often, oh, how often,
  I had wished that the ebbing tide
Would bear me away on its bosom
  O'er the ocean wild and wide!

For my heart was hot and restless,
  And my life was full of care,
And the burden laid upon me
  Seemed greater than I could bear.

But now it has fallen from me,
  It is buried in the sea;
And only the sorrow of others
  Throws its shadow over me.

Yet whenever I cross the river
  On its bridge with wooden piers,
Like the odor of brine from the ocean
  Comes the thought of other years.

And I think how many thousands
  Of care-encumbered men,
Each bearing his burden of sorrow,
  Have crossed the bridge since then.

I see the long procession
  Still passing to and fro,
The young heart hot and restless,
  And the old subdued and slow!

And forever and forever,
  As long as the river flows,
As long as the heart has passions,
  As long as life has woes;

The moon and its broken reflection
  And its shadows shall appear,
As the symbol of love in heaven,
  And its wavering image here.

HOLY, HOLY, HOLY!

Reginald Heber

1783-1826

Bishop Reginald Heber of the Anglican Church was in his late years bishop of Calcutta where he ordained the first native ministers. On April 3, 1826, he officiated in the confirmation of a large group, and under the scorching Indian sun became ill. Retiring to a cold bath, he died within the hour.
This poem has been called the crest of the wave of English hymnology.

Holy, holy, holy, Lord God Almighty!
  Early in the morning our songs shall rise to Thee;
Holy, holy, holy! merciful and mighty!
  God in Three Persons, Blessed Trinity!

Holy, holy, holy! all the saints adore Thee,
  Casting down their golden crowns around the glassy sea;
Cherubim and seraphim falling down before Thee,
  Who wert, and art, and evermore shalt be!

Holy, holy, holy! though the darkness hide Thee,
  Though the eye of sinful man Thy glory may not see,
Only Thou art holy, there is none beside Thee,
  Perfect in power, in love, and purity!

Holy, holy, holy! Lord God Almighty!
  All Thy works shall praise Thy Name, in earth, and sky, and sea;
Holy, holy, holy! merciful and mighty!
  God in Three Persons, Blessèd Trinity!

THERE IS A TIDE

Josephine Johnson

And on the other side
I heard recede the disappointed tide.
      —Emily Dickinson.

    There was an hour when I saw the shore—
    Almost my eager feet had touched the sand;
    Illimitably lovely was the land
    Beyond the breakers and the foam's white roar.
    I stretched my arms—my very heartstrings tore—
    With all my strength I struggled toward the strand—
    But intervening with relentless hand
    Cross currents thrust me back. I could no more.

    Now the tide ebbs and with the undertow
    I am swept ever further out to sea.
    The great waves dash against me, blow by blow,
    But oh, lost land of all felicity—
    Broken, defeated, careless of the night—
    Even in death I hold you in my sight.

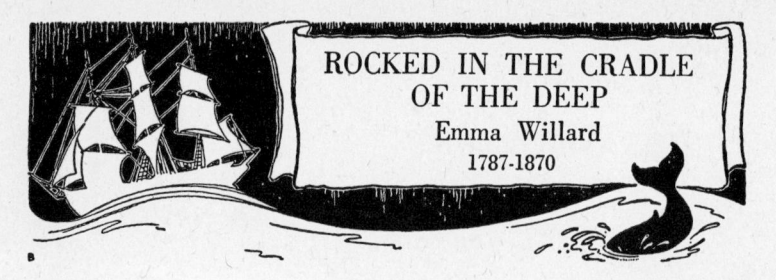

ROCKED IN THE CRADLE OF THE DEEP
Emma Willard
1787-1870

Emma Willard's labors in the field of education for women was recognized in 1905 with her election to the Hall of Fame. She labored in the cause of female education in a day when the wisdom of educating women was a great public question, and she lived to see the beginnings of coeducation.

Rocked in the cradle of the deep
I lay me down in peace to sleep;
Secure I rest upon the wave,
For thou, O Lord, hast power to save.
I know thou wilt not slight my call,
For thou dost mark the sparrow's fall;
And calm and peaceful shall I sleep,
Rocked in the cradle of the deep.

When in the dead of night I lie
And gaze upon the trackless sky,
The star-bespangled heavenly scroll,
The boundless waters as they roll,—
I feel thy wondrous power to save
From perils of the stormy wave:
Rocked in the cradle of the deep
I calmly rest and soundly sleep.

And such the trust that still were mine,
Though stormy winds swept o'er the brine,
Or though the tempest's fiery breath
Roused me from sleep to wreck and death.
In ocean cave still safe with Thee,
The germ of immortality!
And calm and peaceful shall I sleep
Rocked in the cradle of the deep.

THE CHRIST-CHILD
Agnes Lee
1868-

And all the dreams of all the world
Flock to His dreamy eyes.

A woman sings across the wild
A song of wonder sweet,
And everywhere her little Child
Follows her gliding feet.

He flutters like a petal white
Along the roadway's rim;
When He is tired, at latter-light,
His mother carries Him.

Sometimes a little silver star
Floats softly down the air,
Past mountains where the pure snows are,
And sits upon His hair.

Sometimes, when darkness is unfurled,
Upon her breast He lies,
And all the dreams of all the world
Flock to His dreamy eyes.

LIFE
Samuel Johnson
1709-1784

Whose shadow made Boswell famous.

Reflect that life like every other blessing
Derives its value from its use alone.

CHARITY
The Bible

From First Corinthians, Chapter Thirteen.

Though I speak with the tongues of men and of angels,
And have not charity,
I am become as sounding brass or a tinkling cymbal.

And though I have the gift of prophecy,
And understand all mysteries and all knowledge,
And though I have all faith so that I could remove mountains,
And have not charity,
I am nothing.

And though I bestow all my goods to feed the poor,
And though I give my body to be burned,
And have not charity,
It profiteth me nothing.

Charity suffereth long and is kind;

Charity envieth not;
Charity vaunteth not itself, is not puffed up;
Doth not behave itself unseemly,
Seeketh not her own,
Is not easily provoked,
Thinketh no evil;
Rejoiceth not in iniquity but rejoiceth in the truth;

Beareth all things,
Believeth all things,
Hopeth all things,
Endureth all things.

Charity never faileth;

But whether there be prophecies, they shall fail;
Whether there be tongues, they shall cease;
Whether there be knowledge, it shall vanish away.

For we know in part and we prophesy in part;
But when that which is perfect is come,
Then that which is in part shall be done away.

When I was a child, I spake as a child;
I understood as a child,
I thought as a child;
But when I became a man, I put away childish things.

For now we see through a glass darkly,
But then face to face;
Now I know in part,
But then shall I know even as also I am known.

And now abideth faith, hope, charity—
These three,
But the greatest of these is charity.

SO MANY
Frank L. Stanton
1857-

Author of the words "Just a-Wearyin' for You."

So many stars in the infinite space—
So many worlds in the light of God's face.

So many storms ere the thunders shall cease—
So many paths to the portals of peace.

So many years, so many tears—
Sighs and sorrows and pangs and prayers.

So many ships in the desolate night—
So many harbors, and only one Light.

So many creeds like the weeds in the sod—
So many temples, but only one God.

A FOREST HYMN

William Cullen Bryant

1794-1878

Men say the pinnacles of the churches point to heaven; so does every tree that buds and every bird that rises and sings. They say that aisles are good for worship; so is every rough seashore and mountain glen.—Ruskin.

The groves were God's first temples. Ere man learned
To hew the shaft, and lay the architrave,
And spread the roof above them—ere he framed
The lofty vault, to gather and roll back
The sound of anthems; in the darkling wood,
Amid the cool and silence, he knelt down,
And offered to the Mightiest solemn thanks
And supplication. For his simple heart
Might not resist the sacred influence
Which, from the stilly twilight of the place,
And from the gray old trunks that high in heaven
Mingled their mossy bows, and from the sound
Of the invisible breath that swayed at once
All their green tops, stole over him, and bowed
His spirit with the thought of boundless power
And inaccessible majesty. Ah, why
Should we, in the world's riper years, neglect
God's ancient sanctuaries, and adore
Only among the crowd, and under roofs
That our frail hands have raised? Let me, at least,
Here, in the shadow of this aged wood,
Offer one hymn—thrice happy, if it find
Acceptance in His ear.

OLD TEACHER
Gerald Raferty

All over this great land are thousands of men and women who will always remember the honesty and the idealism of certain members of that greatest profession, teaching.

> She has been teaching now for thirty years—
> Has watched each passing generation grow
> And leave her and go on to high careers
> That she will never know.
> When they come back she sees them children yet,
> And smiles to think that others call them men
> Who once were bothered by the alphabet;
> She smiles at them again,
> And never wonders that the world is strange,
> And silly now and then, and full of noise;
> She understands how anything will change
> When run by little boys.

THE ROSARY
Robert Cameron Rogers
1862-1912

The Rosary was written by Robert Cameron Rogers, a Californian, author of Wind in the Clearing, and Other Poems. But it was Ethelbert Nevin's great air that made both men forever famous.

> The hours I spent with thee, dear heart,
>   Are as a string of pearls to me;
> I count them o'er, every one apart,
>   My rosary.

Each hour a pearl, each pearl a prayer,
    To still a heart in absence wrung;
I tell each bead unto the end and there
    A cross is hung.

Oh memories that bless—and burn!
    Oh barren gain—and bitter loss!
I kiss each bead, and strive at last to learn
    To kiss the cross,
        Sweetheart,
            To kiss the cross.

From
SNOWBOUND
John Greenleaf Whittier
1807-1892

Who does not remember:
    The sun that brief December day
    Rose cheerless over hills of gray—
And these two immortal lines—
    That Life is ever lord of Death
    And Love can never lose its own.

O Time and Change!—with hair as gray
As was my sire's that winter day,
How strange it seems, with so much gone
Of life and love, to still live on!
Ah, brother! only I and thou
Are left of all that circle now,—

The dear home faces whereupon
That fitful firelight paled and shone.
Henceforward, listen as we will,
The voices of that hearth are still;
Look where we may, the wide earth o'er,
Those lighted faces smile no more.
We tread the paths their feet have worn,
   We sit beneath their orchard trees,
   We hear, like them, the hum of bees
And rustle of the bladed corn;
We turn the pages that they read,
   Their written words we linger o'er,
But in the sun they cast no shade,
No voice is heard, no sign is made,
   No step is on the conscious floor!
Yet Love will dream and Faith will trust
(Since He who knows our need is just)
That somehow, somewhere, meet we must.
Alas for him who never sees
The stars shine through his cypress-trees!
Who, hopeless, lays his dead away,
Nor looks to see the breaking day
Across the mournful marbles play!
Who hath not learned, in hours of faith,
   The truth to flesh and sense unknown,
That Life is ever lord of Death,
   And Love can never lose its own!

BOUNDARIES

Catherine Cate Coblentz

Man! thou pendulum betwixt a smile and a tear.—Byron.

Man cannot look round the roadway's curve
   Or beyond a mountain see,
And yet he dares to fashion creeds
   And bound eternity.

From SONNET 73

William Shakspere
1564-1616

Joseph Auslander calls these lines "perhaps the greatest of them all." Shakspere directs this sonnet to a beautiful young man, not as yet certainly identified, though often said to be William Herbert, Earl of Pembroke.

> That time of year thou mayest in me behold
> When yellow leaves, or none, or few, do hang
> Upon those boughs which shake against the cold,
> Bare ruin'd choirs where late the sweet birds sang.
> In me thou see'st the twilight of such day
> As after sunset fadeth in the west,
> Which by and by black night doth take away,
> Death's second self, that seals up all in rest.

UPON THE VALLEY'S LAP

Francis William Bourdillon
1852-1921

Francis William Bourdillon, English poet, was the author of lovely little lyrics, the best known of which are The Night Has a Thousand Eyes, and Outwards and Homewards—

> *Oh, weary hearts, that yearn for sleep,*
> *Look, and learn from the ships of the deep.*

> Upon the valley's lap
>   The dewy morning throws
> A thousand pearly drops
>   To wake a single rose.

> So, often in the course
>   Of life's few fleeting years,
> A single pleasure costs
>   The soul a thousand tears.

AS I GROW OLD
Douglas Malloch
1877-

Literature is full of lamentations for oncoming age—Shakspere's "life fallen in the sere, the yellow leaf," and Byron's "The worm, the canker, and the grief are mine alone." How good it is, then, to grow old as grows the western sky.

As I grow old it seems that I
Grow old as grows the western sky
When day is coming to its close:
For life takes on a tint of rose
I had not known in life's hot noon.
Now in the night that comes so soon
I see new stars I had not seen,
A surer faith, a peace serene,
As I grow old.

As I grow old, like men at even,
I turn my eyes again to heaven,
That were so busy with the earth:
And there I find the things of worth,
The things most beautiful of all.
Upon the world shadows fall,
Yet on the world a fairer light,
A golden gleam, a beacon bright,
As I grow old.

As I grow old the winds of life
Die down, the hate, the hurt, the strife.
The waters calm, the waves are still.
I want no triumph, wish no ill
To any man. Now from my heart
The ancient angers all depart.
New friends I know, news songs are sung,
New joys are mine—yes, I grow young
As I grow old!

THE LOST CHORD

Adelaide Proctor
1825-1864

Adelaide Anne Proctor was a daughter of Barry Cornwall [Byron W. Proctor], the poet. This poem she contributed to a London paper where it was seen by Sir Arthur Sullivan while on a train. It so affected him that he composed the air we know and hurried home to set it down.

> Seated one day at the organ,
>   I was weary and ill at ease,
> And my fingers wandered idly
>   Over the noisy keys.
>
> I do not know what I was playing,
>   Or what I was dreaming then;
> But I struck one chord of music,
>   Like the sound of a great Amen.
>
> It flooded the crimson twilight
>   Like the close of an Angel's Psalm,
> And it lay on my fevered spirit
>   With a touch of infinite calm.
>
> It quieted pain and sorrow,
>   Like love overcoming strife;
> It seemed the harmonious echo
>   From our discordant life.
>
> It linked all perplexèd meanings
>   Into one perfect peace,
> And trembled away into silence,
>   As if it were loth to cease.

[52]

I have sought, but I seek it vainly,
    That one lost chord divine,
Which came from the soul of the organ,
    And entered into mine.

It may be that Death's bright angel
    Will speak in that chord again,—
It may be that only in Heaven
    I shall hear that grand Amen.

VICTORY

Anonymous

The following lines were found upon the body of a slain Australian soldier in the Great War. The pathetic hope, that from the killing of men, others "might see the morning break," is but the age-old treachery of justifying inhumanity by humane ends. Would that we had really seen "the morning break."

Ye that have faith to look with fearless eyes
    Beyond the tragedy of a world at strife,
And know that out of death and night shall rise
    The dawn of ampler life:
Rejoice, whatever anguish rend the heart,
    That God has given you the priceless dower
To live in these great times and have your part
    In Freedom's crowning hour,
That ye may tell your sons who see the light
    High in the heavens—their heritage to take—
"I saw the powers of darkness take their flight;
    I saw the morning break."

A PAGE FROM AMERICA'S PSALTER
Willard Wattles
1888-

> *Too long we have delayed in putting the call for social justice squarely on the tenets of Christianity. It is not the teachings of Christ but selfishness and wilful blindness to His messages of mercy that makes our countless thousands mourn.*

Across the bitter centuries I hear the wail of men:
"Oh, would that Jesus Lord, the Christ, would come to us again."
We decorate our altars with a ceremonious pride,
With all the outward shows of pomp His worship is supplied:
Great churches raise their mighty spires to pierce the sunlit skies
While in the shadow of the cross we mutter blasphemies.

We know we do not do His will who lessoned us to pray,
"Our Father grant within our lives Thy Kingdom rule today."
The prayer He taught us once a week we mouth with half-shut eye
While in the charnel-house of words immortal meanings die.
Above our brothers' frailties we cry "Unclean! Unclean!"
And with the hands that served her shame still stone the Magdalene.

We know within our factories that wan-cheeked women reel
Among the deft and droning belts that spin from wheel to wheel.
We know that unsexed childhood droops in dull-eyed drudgery—
The little children that He blessed in far off Galilee,—
Yet, surely, Lord, our hearts would grow more merciful to them,
If Thou couldst come again to us as once in Bethlehem.

WHEN GOD THOUGHT OF YOU

George MacDonald

1824-1905

I want to help you to grow as beautiful as God meant you to be when He thought of you first.

THE CHRIST OF COMMON FOLKS
George T. Liddell

If our love were but more simple, we should take Him at His word, and our lives would be all sunshine in the sweetness of the Lord.—Faber.

I love the name of Christ the Lord, the man of Galilee,
Because he came to live and toil among the likes of me.
Let others sing the praises of a mighty King of kings;
I love the Christ of common folks, the Lord of common things.

The beggars and the feeble ones, the poor and sick and blind,
The wayward and the tempted ones, were those he loved to find;
He lived with them to help them like a brother and a friend,
Or like some wandering workman finding things to mend.

I know my Lord is still my kind of folks to this good day;
I know because he never fails to hear me when I pray.
He loves the people that he finds in narrow dingy streets,
And brings a word of comfort to the weary one he meets.

My job is just a poor man's job, my home is just a shack,
But on my humble residence he has never turned his back.
Let others sing their praises to a mighty King of kings;
I love the Christ of common folks, the Lord of common things.

NO WORD OF FEAR
Walter Savage Landor
1775-1864

Fear is more painful to cowardice than death to true courage.
—Sir Philip Sidney.

Death stands above me, whispering low
    I know not what into my ear;
Of his strange language all I know
    Is, there is not a word of fear.

BLACK SHEEP
Richard Burton
1859-

Richard Eugene Burton, sometime managing editor of The Churchman, and successively professor of literature in the universities of Minnesota and Chicago, pleads for the misunderstanding and the misunderstood.

From their folded mates they wander far,
    Their ways seem harsh and wild;
They follow the beck of a baleful star,
    Their paths are dream beguiled.

Yet haply they sought but a wider range,
    Some loftier mountain-slope,
And little recked of the country strange
    Beyond the gates of hope.

And haply a bell with a luring call
    Summoned their feet to tread
Midst the cruel rocks, where the deep pitfall
    And the lurking snare are spread.

Maybe, in spite of their tameless days
    Of outcast liberty,
They're sick at heart for the homely ways
    Where their gathered brothers be.

And oft at night, when the plains fall dark
    And the hills loom large and dim,
For the Shepherd's voice they mutely hark,
    And their souls go out to him.

Meanwhile, "Black sheep! Black sheep!" we cry,
    Safe in the inner fold;
And maybe they hear, and wonder why,
    And marvel, out in the cold.

MY MINDE TO ME
A KINGDOM IS

William Byrd

1538?-1623

This great poem was written about the time of the first settlement of America—that is, more than three centuries ago. But take it stanza for stanza and you will find it familiarly modern, so little have the centuries changed the equity of man's relations with man.
Byrd was organist to Queen Elizabeth.

My minde to me a kingdom is;
   Such perfect joy therein I finde
As farre exceeds all earthly blisse
   That God or Nature hath assignde;
Though much I want, that most would have,
Yet still my minde forbids to crave.

Content I live; this is my stay—
   I seek no more than may suffice.
I presse to beare no haughtie sway;
   Look, what I lack my minde supplies.
Loe, thus I triumph like a king,
Content with that my minde doth bring.

I see how plentie surfets oft,
   And hastie clymbers soonest fall;
I see that such as sit aloft
   Mishap doth threaten most of all.
These get with toile, and keepe with feare:
Such cares my minde could never beare.

Some have too much, yet still they crave;
   I little have, yet seek no more.

They are but poore, though much they have,
   And I am rich with little store.
They poor, I rich; they beg, I give;
They lacke, I lend; they pine, I live.

I laugh not at another's losse,
   I grudge not at another's gaine;
No worldly wave my minde can tosse;
   I brooke that is another's bane.
I feare no foe, nor fawne on friend;
I lothe not life, nor dread mine end.

I kisse not where I wish to kill;
   I feign not love where most I hate;
I breake no sleepe to winne my will;
   I wayte not at the mightie's fate.
I scorne no poore, I feare no rich;
I feel no want, nor have too much.

My wealth is health and perfect ease;
   My conscience clere my chiefe defence;
I never seek by bribes to please,
   Nor by desert to give offence.
Thus do I live, thus will I die;
Would all did so as well as I!

'TAIN'T

From the Log, United States Naval Academy
An' you can't say 'tain't so!

'Tain't what we have
   But what we give;
'Tain't where we are,
   But how we live;
'Tain't what we do,
   But how we do it —
That makes this life
   Worth goin' through it.

FARMERS
William Alexander Percy
1885-

*And the land shall yield her increase, and the trees of the field shall yield their fruit.
And isn't it really true that the farmer's work is done "in partnership with Him?"*

I watch the farmers in their fields
    And marvel secretly.
They are so very calm and sure,
    They have such dignity.

They know such simple things so well,
    Although their learning's small,
They find a steady, brown content
    Where some find none at all.

And all their quarrelings with God
    Are soon made up again;
They grant forgiveness when He sends
    His silver, tardy rain.

Their pleasure is so grave and full
    When gathered crops are trim,
You know they think their work was done
    In partnership with Him.

Then, why, when there are fields to buy,
    And little fields to rent,
Do I still love so foolishly
    Wisdom and discontent?

JESUS, SAVIOUR, PILOT ME
Edward Hopper
1818-

One of the greatest hymns, and one of the finest poems in the English language. Edward Hopper was for years pastor of the Presbyterian Church of Sea and Land, in New York City. The beat of the inexorable sea is in the verse, and an unquestioning reliance on the Pilot.

I hope to see my Pilot face to face,
When I have crossed the bar.
—Tennyson.

Jesus, Saviour, pilot me,
Over life's tempestuous sea;
Unknown waves before me roll,
Hiding rock and treacherous shoal;
Chart and compass came from thee:
Jesus, Saviour, pilot me.

As a mother stills her child,
Thou canst hush the ocean wild;
Boisterous waves obey thy will
When thou say'st to them "Be still!"
Wondrous Sovereign of the sea
Jesus, Saviour, pilot me.

When at last I near the shore,
And the fearful breakers roar
'Twixt me and the peaceful rest,
Then, while leaning on thy breast,
May I hear thee say to me,
"Fear not, I will pilot thee!"

JOSHUA PEABODY
John A. Holmes

No snow falls lighter than the snow of age; but none lies heavier, for it never melts.

When Joshua Peabody drives to town
   His route is always the same:
Comes in by the Peabody turnpike road,
   Named for his family's name,
Waters his horse at the watering trough
   And drives to the village store,
Buys what he bought last time he came,
   Not one bit less or more,
Goes to the postoffice after mail
   (There's never any there)
And then to his brother Arthur's house
   Just outside of the square;
Passes a word and the time of day,
   Then jerks his horse's rein,
Goes out by the Peabody turnpike road
   And so back home again.
But just outside of the village line
   Is the village burying ground,
And there he stops, goes in, and kneels
   Near a little grassy mound,
And places some flowers he brought from home
   Near the headstone standing there.
And then his tired old trembling lips
   Move in a silent prayer

For the wife who died twelve years ago,
  All that he loved on earth.
Then heavily goes where the buggy waits,
  Tightens the harness girth,
And drives on home to his lowly house,
  Little and quiet and brown,
And lives on slowly through the days
  Till next he comes to town.

MARY MAGDALEN
Richard Burton
1861-

Jesus sayeth unto her, Mary. She turned herself, and saith unto him, Rabboni; which is to say, Master.—St. John XX. 16.

At dawn she sought the Saviour slain,
To kiss the spot where He had lain
And weep warm tears, like spring-time rain;

When lo, there stood, unstained of death,
A man that spoke with low sweet breath;
And "Master!" Mary answereth.

From out the far and fragrant years
How sweeter than the songs of seers
That tender offering of tears!

SAVED BY GRACE
Fanny Crosby
1820-1915

Frances Jane Crosby (Mrs. Alexander Van Alstyne) became blind from improper medical care while yet a child. At fifteen she entered the Institute for the Blind, in New York, and stayed on to become a teacher. She began as a popular song writer (Hazel Dell, and Rosalie the Prairie Flower) but turned to religious music. Her best known songs include, Rescue the Perishing, Pass Me Not O Gentle Saviour, and There's Music in the Air.

> Some day the silver cord will break
>   And I no more as now shall sing;
> But Oh, the joy when I shall wake
>   Within the palace of the King!
>
> *And I shall see Him face to face,*
> *And tell the story—Saved by Grace.*
>
> Some day my earthly house will fall;
>   I cannot tell how soon 'twill be;
> But this I know—my All in All
>   Has now a place in heav'n for me.
>
> Some day, when fades the golden sun
>   Beneath the rosy-tinted west,
> My blessed Lord will say, "Well done!"
>   And I will enter into rest.
>
> Some day; till then I'll watch and wait,
>   My lamp all trimmed and burning,
> That when my bright Saviour ope's the gate,
>   My soul to Him may take its flight.

TO THE WORLD'S EDGE
Donn Byrne
1889-1928

A song of lightness—for life, too, is often a-weary of the sobbing of the great white sea.

I will take my pipes and go now, for the bees upon the sill
Are singing of the summer that is coming from the stars.
I will take my pipes and go now, for the little mountain rill
Is pleading with the bagpipes in tender, crooning bars.

I will go o'er hills and valleys, and through fields of ripening rye,
And the linnet and the throstle and the bittern in the sedge
Will hush their throats and listen, as the piper passes by
On the great long road of silver that ends at the world's edge.

I will take my pipes and go now, for the sand-flower on the dunes
Is a-weary of the sobbing of the great white sea,
And is asking for the piper, with his basketful of tunes,
To play the merry lilting that sets all hearts free.

I will take my pipes and go now, and God go with you all,
And keep all sorrow from you, and the dark heart's load;
I will take my pipes and go now, for I hear the summer call,
And you'll hear the pipes a-singing as I pass along the road.

CONSCIENCE
William Shakspere
1564-1616

From Lucrece, 1342

They whose guilt within their bosom lies
Imagine every eye beholds their blame.

THE IVY GREEN
Charles Dickens
1812-1870

Ivy and castle walls seem to have been favorites of Dickens, for during the last day of his life he expressed a wish to be buried beneath the walls of Rochester Cathedral, of "surpassing beauty with the lusty ivy gleaming in the sun."

He was buried in stately Westminster Abbey. Will it ever be there that—

> *The stateliest building man can raise*
> *Is the Ivy's food at last.*

Oh, a dainty plant is the Ivy green,
    That creepeth o'er ruins old!
Of right choice food are his meals I ween,
    In his cell so lone and cold.
The wall must be crumbled, the stone decayed,
    To pleasure his dainty whim;
And the mouldering dust that years have made
    Is a merry meal for him.
        Creeping where no life is seen,
        A rare old plant is the Ivy green.

Fast he stealeth on, though he wears no wings,
    And a staunch old heart has he,
How closely he twineth, how tight he clings,
    To his friend the huge Oak Tree!
And slyly he traileth along the ground,
    And his leaves he gently waves,
As he joyously hugs and crawleth round
    The rich mould of dead men's graves.
        Creeping where grim death has been,
        A rare old plant is the Ivy green.

Whole ages have fled and their works decayed,
   And nations have scattered been;
But the stout old Ivy shall never fade
   From its hale and hearty green.
The brave old plant, in its lonely days,
   Shall fatten upon the past:
For the stateliest building man can raise
   Is the Ivy's food at last.
     Creeping on where time has been,
     A rare old plant is the Ivy green.

THE HARVEST WAITS
Lloyd Mifflin
1846-1921

Lloyd Mifflin, a portrait painter, was the son of a portrait painter. The son, however, abandoned painting for poetry. Few things that he has written will live; but The Harvest Waits is so full of the painter's imagery, and so condensed of phrase, made the more so by the rigidity of his theology, that lovers of poetry will read it for the thrill of its powerful strophes.

God hath been patient long. In eons past
   He plowed the waste of Chaos. He hath sown
   The furrows with His worlds, and from His throne
Showered, like grain, planets upon the Vast.
What meed of glory hath He from the past?
   Shall He not reap, who hears but prayer and groan?
   The harvest waits . . . He cometh to His own,—
He who shall scythe the starry host at last.
When the accumulated swarms of Death
   Glut the rank worlds as rills are choked with leaves,
   Then shall God flail the million orbs, as sheaves
   Unfruitful gleaned; and, in His age sublime,
Winnow the gathered stars, and with a breath
   Whirl the spurned chaff adown the void of Time.

ABIDE WITH ME
Henry Francis Lyte
1793-1847

Henry Francis Lyte was born in Scotland but educated in Trinity College, Dublin. He was ordained in 1815 and somewhat later sent to Lower Brixham, a fishing village on the coast of Devonshire. He seems to have lamented the short opportunities for one of literary inclinations among his simple but obstinate fisher folk. He served them faithfully, we would know from reading his great hymns, until failing health forced him to a final communion service, after which he mumbled a blessing and retired to his room. And then in the shadows of a Devonshire Sabbath evening, he wrote his farewell song, Abide With Me. He died on his way to Rome and is buried at Nice. But no monument will outlast his hymn.

Abide with me! Fast falls the eventide;
The darkness deepens; Lord, with me abide!
When other helpers fail, and comforts flee,
Help of the helpless, O abide with me!

Swift to its close ebbs out life's little day;
Earth's joys grow dim, its glories pass away:
Change and decay in all around I see;
O Thou, who changest not, abide with me!

Not a brief glance, I beg, a passing word,
But as Thou dwell'st with Thy disciples, Lord,
Familiar, condescending, patient, free,
Come, not to sojourn, but abide, with me.

Come not in terrors, as the King of kings;
But kind and good, with healing in Thy wings,
Tears for all woes, a heart for every plea;
Come, Friend of sinners, and abide with me.

[67]

Thou on my head in early youth didst smile,
And, though rebellious and perverse meanwhile,
Thou hast not left me, oft as I left Thee:
On to the close, O Lord, abide with me!

I need Thy presence every passing hour.
What but Thy grace can foil the tempter's power?
Who like Thyself my guide and stay can be?
Through cloud and sunshine, O abide with me!

I fear no foe, with Thee at hand to bless:
Ills have no weight, and tears no bitterness.
Where is death's sting, where, grave, thy victory?
I triumph still, if Thou abide with me.

Hold then Thy cross before my closing eyes,
Shine through the gloom, and point me to the skies;
Heaven's morning breaks and earth's vain shadows flee:
In life, in death, O Lord, abide with me!

VESPERAL
Silas Weir Mitchell
1829-1914

Dr. Silas Weir Mitchell was a famous physician as well as a man of literature. His writings cover a wide field from medical practice to poetry and the novel, the best known being Hugh Wynne, Free Quaker, a story of the Revolution.

I know the night is near at hand.
The mists lie low on hill and bay,
The autumn sheaves are dewless, dry;
But I have had the day.

Yes, I have had, dear Lord, the day;
When at Thy call I have the night,
Brief be the twilight as I pass
From light to dark, from dark to light.

THE SEEKERS
Victor Starbuck
1887-1935

If God hath made this world so fair, where sin and death abound, how beautiful beyond compare will paradise be found.
—*Montgomery.*

One asked a sign from God; and day by day
The sun arose in pearl, in scarlet set,
Each night the stars appeared in bright array,
Each morn the thirsting grass with dew was wet.
The corn failed not its harvest, nor the vine.
And yet he saw no sign.

One longed to hear a prophet; and he strayed
Through crowded streets, and by the open sea.
He saw men send their ships for distant trade,
And build for generations yet to be.
He saw the farmer sow his acres wide,
But went unsatisfied.

One prayed a sight of heaven; and erewhile
He saw a workman at his noontime rest.
He saw one dare for honor, and the smile
Of one who held a babe upon her breast;
At dusk two lovers walking hand in hand;
But did not understand.

FOR ONE WHO DIED

Jessica Powers

Under the crosses white on a foreign meadow
Mute they are lying who marched in the spring-sweet sun.
Nothing is here of the life, the joy, the loving,
Before a war was won.
  —Catherine Parmenter.

He sleeps somewhere beneath the sod in France,
I think not even the angels know just where,
And there is only the candlelight of stars
  And sobbing winds to care.

I cannot deck his grave with wreaths of love,
Nor little songs, nor flowers of sunset skies,
Nor tell above him any beads of prayer,
  Who know not where he lies!

O May, smother his bed in flowers for me,
Sing him a requiem when stars are dim,
And tell him all your beauty and your love
  Is my heart's gift to him!

SILENCE

Charles Hanson Towne

1877-

Nature is the visible garment of God.—Goethe.

I need not shout my faith. Thrice eloquent
Are quiet trees and the green listening sod;
Hushed are the stars, whose power is never spent;
The hills are mute: yet how they speak of God!

THE POET
Witter Bynner
1881-

This is a lovely and gentle poem by a poet who is known for his passion for democracy and for honesty in literature.

A poet lived in Galilee,
Whose mother dearly knew him—
And his beauty like a cooling tree
Drew many people to him.

He loved the speech of simple men
And little children's laughter,
He came—they always came again,
He went—they followed after.

He had sweet-hearted things to say,
And he was solemn only
When people were unkind . . . that day
He would stand there straight and lonely

And tell them what they ought to do:
"Love other folk," he pleaded,
"As you love me and I love you!"
But almost no one heeded.

A poet died in Galilee,
They stared at him and slew him . . .
What would they do to you and me
If we could say we knew him?

THE ANVIL

Anonymous

Nobody ever outgrows Scripture; the book widens and deepens with our years.
—*Spurgeon.*

Last eve I passed beside a blacksmith's door,
  And heard the anvil ring the vesper chime;
Then looking in, I saw upon the floor
  Old hammers, worn with beating years of time.

"How many anvils have you had," said I,
  "To wear and batter all these hammers so?"
"Just one," said he, and then, with twinkling eye,
  "The anvil wears the hammers out, you know."

And so, thought I, the anvil of God's Word,
  For ages skeptic blows have beat upon;
Yet, though the noise of falling blows was heard,
  The anvil is unharmed—the hammers gone.

LORD, TAKE AWAY PAIN

Anonymous

The mark of rank in nature is capacity for pain.—Sarah Williams.

The cry of man's anguish went up unto God,
  "Lord, take away pain!—
The shadow that darkens the world Thou hast made;
  The close-coiling chain
That strangles the heart; the burden that weighs
  On the wings that would soar—
Lord, take away pain from the world Thou hast made,
  That it love Thee the more!"

Then answered the Lord to the cry of His world:
  "Shall I take away pain,
And with it the power of the soul to endure,
  Made strong by the strain?
Shall I take away pity, that knits heart to heart,
  And sacrifice high?
Will ye lose all your heroes that lift from the fire
  White brows to the sky?
Shall I take away love, that redeems with a price,
  And smiles at its loss?
Can you spare from your lives that would climb unto mine,
  The Christ on his cross?"

MY NEIGHBOR
Virginia Eaton

How beautiful can time with goodness make an old man look.—Jerrold.

He needs must work, though time's onrushing wings
Have left bright bits of soft down in his hair;
His gnarled old hands will potter with such things
As rake and hoe, or with painstaking care
He builds a rustic seat beneath the trees;
He cuts the lawn and clips the edges trim.
In simple daily labors such as these
He keeps an independence dear to him.

He who has always worked is not content
With idle hours; all toil to him is sweet.
He counts that day as lost, at least ill-spent,
That sees no labor of the hands complete.
Dear God, when he walks shining ways with You,
Please give his eager hands some work to do.

STAINS

Theodosia Garrison
1874-

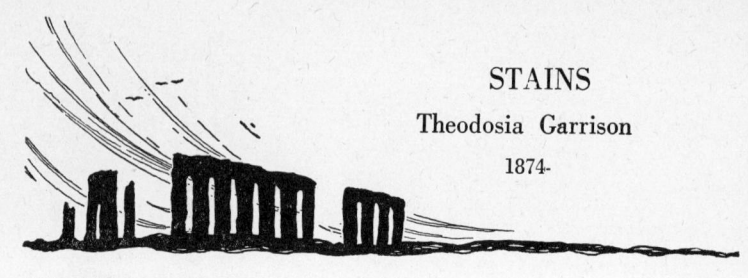

Naked the soul goes up to God.

The three ghosts on the lonesome road,
    Spake each to one another,
"Whence came that stain about your mouth
    No lifted hand may cover?"
"From eating of forbidden fruit,
    Brother, my brother."

The three ghosts on the sunless road
    Spake each to one another,
"Whence came that red burn on your feet
    No dust or ash may cover?"
"I stamped a neighbor's heart-flame out,
    Brother, my brother."

The three ghosts on the windless road
    Spake each to one another,
"Whence came that blood upon your hand
    No other hand may cover?"
"From breaking of a woman's heart,
    Brother, my brother."

"Yet on the earth clean men we walked,
    Glutton and Thief and Lover;
White flesh and fair it hid our stains
    That no man might discover."
"Naked the soul goes up to God,
    Brother, my brother."

PRAYER

Gertie Stewart Phillips

Heaven is never deaf but when man's heart is dumb.—Quarles.

Oftimes I pray with words;
Or else just close my eyes
And listen to rapt birds
Petitioning the skies
With song; once a deep flood
Of reverence drowned my woes
When a jade-sheathed bud
Unpetaled to a rose.
And when my lips would pray
In a soft-lighted church,
They found no words to say;
Strangely, outside, a birch,
So like an angel there
With wings bent to the wind,
Murmured a truant prayer
My dumb lips could not find.
Bells chiming hymns I knew
Were silvery as the tree
O'ershadowing a pew
Wherein God knelt with me.

WE VISIT MY ESTATE

Richard R. Kirk

That cloud, now! Just below that strip of blue!
You like it? That's mine too!

THE CHRISTMAS CALF
Judy Van der Veer

This lovely little poem is typical of modern poetry, simple, unaffected, accurate, and of the common cloth of living.

The cows are milked, the horses fed;
   And nestled in the sweet warm hay,
There sleeps a little spotted calf
   Born early on this Christmas day.

I found it when I came to milk,
   Before the stars had left the sky;
Its mother standing over it,
   With deep and watchful eye.

And though the wind outside was cold,
   The big barn was a kindly place;
I moved my lantern back and forth
   And saw it light each creature's face.

I pitched down hay and thought how good
   And sweet a place a barn may be;
I heard the pigeons move about
   On rafters where I could not see.

The barn was filled with sound of wings
   As pigeons wakened into flight;
And then I thought of Angel wings
   Above a barn one Holy Night...

Of barns made sacred by a Child
   Who came to bless all helpless things—
(The little spotted calf slept on,
   All unaware of shining wings.)

THE NINETY AND NINE
Mrs. Elizabeth C. Clephane
1830-1869

Ira David Sankey, the musical partner of the great Moody and Sankey team, was in one of his famous meetings in Edinburgh, Scotland, one night in 1874. Moody had just preached a stirring sermon on the Good Shepherd, and Sankey was called upon to sing. "Sing the hymn you found on the train" an inner voice seemed to say. It was The Ninety and Nine, by Elizabeth Clephane, a native of Scotland. There was as yet no music; but at this intense moment Sankey arose and with eyes set upon the verses, at once composed and sang the song that made him famous.

There were ninety and nine that safely lay
   In the shelter of the fold;
But one was out on the hills away,
   Far off from the gates of gold,—
Away on the mountains wild and bare,
Away from the tender Shepherd's care.

"Lord, thou hast here thy ninety and nine:
   Are they not enough for thee?
But the Shepherd made answer: "This of mine
   Has wandered away from me;
And although the road be rough and steep
I go to the desert to find my sheep."

But none of the ransomed ever knew
   How deep were the waters crossed,
Nor how dark was the night that the Lord passed through
   Ere he found his sheep that was lost.
Out in the desert he heard its cry,—
Sick and helpless, and ready to die.

"Lord, whence are those blood-drops all the way,
   That mark out the mountain-track?"
"They were shed for one who had gone astray
   Ere the Shepherd could bring him back."

"Lord, whence are thy hands so rent and torn?"
"They are pierced tonight by many a thorn."

But all through the mountains, thunder-riven,
   And up from the rocky steep,
There rose a cry to the gate of heaven,
    "Rejoice! I have found my sheep!"
And the angels echoed around the throne
"Rejoice, for the Lord brings back His own!"

WHERE RUNS THE RIVER
Francis William Bourdillon
1852-1921

Francis William Bourdillon was an English scholar, poet, and teacher. He is best remembered by his lovely lyrics. But not even The Night Has a Thousand Eyes surpasses Where Runs the River.

Where runs the river? Who can say
Who hath not followed all the way
By alders green and sedges gray
    And blossoms blue?

Where runs the river? Hill and wood
Curve round to hem the eager flood;
It cannot straightly as it would
    Its path pursue.

Yet this we know: O'er whatso plains
Or rocks or waterfalls it strains,
At last the vast the stream attains;
    And I, and you.

THE TRUE BIBLE
Sam Walter Foss
1858-1911

It is one of the strongest proofs of an evolution on to eternity that we find so much joy in going on to better things. Why should progress give us joy, unless it is that we thereby approach the ultimate Good?

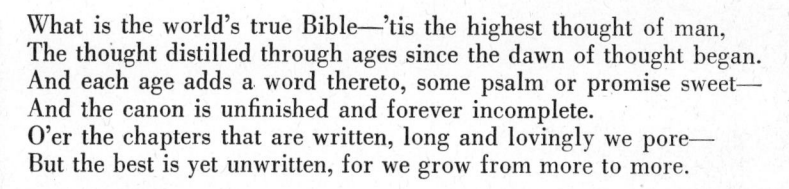

What is the world's true Bible—'tis the highest thought of man,
The thought distilled through ages since the dawn of thought began.
And each age adds a word thereto, some psalm or promise sweet—
And the canon is unfinished and forever incomplete.
O'er the chapters that are written, long and lovingly we pore—
But the best is yet unwritten, for we grow from more to more.

Let us heed the voice within us and its messages rehearse;
Let us build the growing Bible—for we too must write a verse.
What is the purport of the scheme toward which all time is gone?
What is the great aeonian goal? The joy of going on.

And are there any souls so strong, such feet with swiftness shod,
That they shall reach it, reach some bourne, the ultimate of God?
There is no bourne, no ultimate. The very farthest star
But rims a sea of other stars that stretches just as far.
There's no beginning and no end: As in the ages gone,
The greatest joy of joys shall be—the joy of going on.

OUR DAILY BREAD
Maltbie D. Babcock
1858-1901

Back of the loaf is the snowy flour,
    And back of the flour the mill;
And back of the mill is the wheat, and the shower,
    And the sun, and the Father's will.

I LOVE TO STEAL AWHILE AWAY

Phoebe Brown

1783-1861

Mrs. Brown's fame rests entirely on this one sincere, tender poem. It reflects the manner of her own life; for, an orphan, she was early forced to work about a New York county jail, and after the conditions of the day, to see and endure unspeakable things. From such misery this retiring tired little life found peace in prayer. Her son was the first American missionary to Japan.

I love to steal awhile away
    From every cumbering care,
And spend the hours of setting day
    In humble, grateful prayer.

I love in solitude to shed
    The penitential tear,
And all his promises to plead,
    Where none but God can hear.

I love to think on mercies past,
    And future good implore,
And all my cares and sorrows cast
    On him whom I adore.

I love by faith to take a view
    Of brighter scenes in heaven;
The prospect doth my strength renew,
    While here by tempest driven.

Thus, when life's toilsome day is o'er,
    May its departing ray
Be calm as this impressive hour,
    And lead to endless day.

O YET WE TRUST
Alfred Tennyson
1809-1892

The ultimate Tennyson, often fearful that the broad daylight of science might obscure softer spiritual values, downcast that men must so long remain in their ignorance and misery, comes out in a poem like this from In Memoriam.

>O yet we trust that somehow good
> Will be the final goal of ill,
> To pangs of nature, sins of will,
>Defects of doubt, and taints of blood;
>
>That nothing walks with aimless feet;
> That not one life shall be destroy'd,
> Or cast as rubbish to the void,
>When God hath made the pile complete;
>
>That not a worm is cloven in vain;
> That not a moth with vain desire
> Is shrivell'd in a fruitless fire,
>Or but subserves another's gain.
>
>Behold we know not anything;
> I can but trust that good shall fall
> At last—far off—at last, to all,
>And every winter change to spring.

GOOD IN EVERYTHING
William Shakspere
1564-1616

From As You Like It. 2:1, 16.

>And this our life, exempt from public haunt
>Finds tongues in trees, books in running brooks,
>Sermons in stones, and good in everything.

INDIFFERENCE

G. A. Studdert-Kennedy

The Reverend G. A. Studdert Kennedy, a poet of note, is chaplain to His Majesty, The King of England.

When Jesus came to Golgotha they
    hanged Him on a tree,
They drave great nails through
    hands and feet, and made a Calvary;
They crowned Him with a crown of thorns,
    red were His wounds and deep,
For those were crude and cruel days,
    and human flesh was cheap.

When Jesus came to Birmingham
    they simply passed Him by,
They never hurt a hair of Him,
    they only let Him die;
For men had grown more tender,
    and they would not give Him pain,
They only just passed down the street,
    and left Him in the rain.

Still Jesus cried, "Forgive them,
    for they know not what they do,"
And still it rained the Winter rain
    that drenched Him through and through;
The crowds went home and left the
    streets without a soul to see,
And Jesus crouched against a wall
    and cried for Calvary.

WHY SHOULD WE MOURN?
Anonymous

The silence often of pure innocence
Persuades when speaking fails.
    —*The Winter's Tale, 2:2, 41.*

It sometimes happens that two friends will meet,
    And, with a smile and touch of hands, again
Go on their way along the noisy street.
Each is so sure of all the friendship sweet,
    The loving silence gives no thought of pain.

And so, I think those friends whom we call dead
Are with us. It may be some quiet hour,
Or time of busy work for hand or head—
Their love fills all the heart that missed them so.
They bring a sweet assurance of the life
Serene, above the worry that we know;
    And we grow braver for the comfort brought.
Why should we mourn because they do not speak
Our words that lie so far below their thought?

THE GOOD FIGHT
William Cullen Bryant
1794-1878

The last four lines are among the most famous in English literature. Almost everyone knows them but few know they were written by Bryant.

    Yet nerve thy spirit to the proof,
        And blench not at thy chosen lot;
    The timid good may stand aloof,
        The sage may frown,—yet faint thou not

    Nor heed the shaft too surely cast,
        The foul and hissing bolt of scorn;
    For with thy side shall dwell, at last,
        The victory of endurance born.

Truth, crushed to earth, shall rise again—
The eternal years of God are hers;
But error, wounded, writhes in pain,
And dies among her worshippers.

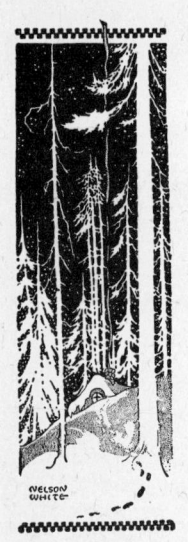

O GOD, OUR HELP IN AGES PAST
Isaac Watts
1674-1748

On the last day of life, Matthew Arnold attended the Sefton Park Church in Liverpool, of which Dr. John Watson ("Ian Maclaren") was pastor. That evening at lunch he was heard to repeat the opening lines of O God, Our Help in Ages Past, with the statement that they were the greatest in the language. He died a few minutes later.

O God, our help in ages past,
  Our hope in years to come,
Our shelter from the stormy blast,
  And our eternal home—

Under the shadow of Thy throne
  Thy saints have dwelt secure;
Sufficient is Thine arm alone,
  And our defense is sure.

Before the hills in order stood,
  Or earth received her frame,
From everlasting Thou art God,
  To endless years the same.

A thousand ages in Thy sight
  Are like an evening gone;
Short as the watch that ends the night
  Before the rising sun.

Time, like the ever-rolling stream
  Bears all its sons away;
They fly, forgotten, as a dream
  Dies at the opening day.

O God, our help in ages past,
  Our hope in years to come,
Be thou our guard while troubles last,
  And our eternal home.

EPIGRAM
Sir William Watson
1858-1934

Eight lines from a great British poet whose memory doth remain:
Captains and conquerors leave a little dust,
  And kings a dubious record of their reign;
The swords of Caesars, they are less than rust:
  The poet doth remain.

When whelmed are altar, priest and creed;
  When all the faiths are passed;
Perhaps from darkening incense freed,
  God may emerge at last.

"MY HEART LEAPS UP"
William Wordsworth
1770-1850

When a visitor asked to be shown Wordsworth's study, a servant replied, "Here is his library, but his study is out of doors."

My heart leaps up when I behold
  A rainbow in the sky:
So was it when my life began;
So is it now I am a man;
So be it when I shall grow old,
  Or let me die!
The Child is father of the Man;
And I could wish my days to be
Bound each to each by natural piety.

THE RUSTLE OF A WING

Robert G. Ingersoll

1833-1899

Robert Green Ingersoll, whose name during the last half of the nineteenth century, was generally synonymous with Beelzebub, was unusually kind and tender. While he attacked creeded religions, there is evidence that he revered the Great Cause: else why should he have uttered these words at the grave of his brother, January 3, 1879?

> Life is a narrow vale
> Between the barren peaks
>   Of two eternities.
>
> We strive in vain to look beyond the heights
> We cry aloud and the only answer
>   Is the echo of our wailing cry.
> From the voiceless lips
> Of the unreplying dead
>   There comes no answer.
>
> But in the night of death
> Hope sees a star,
> And listening love
> Can hear the rustle of a wing.

DOOR-MATS

Mary Caroline Davies

Sam Jones, the preacher, used to say that if the men don't reform there won't be enough in heaven to sing bass. But perhaps with the aid of the door-mats there may be more help in the choir.

> Women are door-mats and have been,—
>   The years those mats applaud,—
> They keep their men from going in
>   With muddy feet to God.

IMMANENCE

Anonymous

Till the bridge you will need be form'd, till the ductile anchor hold;
Till the gossamer thread you fling, catch somewhere O my Soul.
—*Walt Whitman.*

My thoughts go out like spider-threads,
   Cast forth upon the air,
Filmy and fine, and floating wide,
Caught by whatever may betide,
   To seek Thee everywhere.

In league with every breeze that blows,
   All ways, all holds they dare;
North, east, or south, or west they fly,
And sure, though winds be low or high,
   To find Thee everywhere.

Love still is lord of space and fate:
   All roads his runners fare;
All heights that bar, they laughing climb;
They find all days the fitting time,
   And highways everywhere.

THE DAYS

Theodosia Garrison

Theodosia Garrison (Mrs. Frederick J. Faulks) is the author of much lovely poetry.

I call my years back, I, grown old,
   Recall them day by day;
And some are dressed in cloth o' gold
   And some in humble gray.

And those in gold glance scornfully
Or pass me unawares;
But those in gray come close to me
And take my hand in theirs.

MY FAITH LOOKS UP TO THEE

Ray Palmer

1808-1887

This hymn was written in 1830 when the author was but twenty-two, and evidently for himself, for it was only at the request of Dr. Lowell Mason that it was published. Dr. Benson says of it, "It seems to many people like a part of their own spiritual life."

My faith looks up to thee,
Thou Lamb of Calvary,
    Saviour divine!
Now hear me while I pray,
Take all my guilt away,
Oh, let me from this day
    Be wholly thine!

May thy rich grace impart
Strength to my fainting heart;
    My zeal inspire;
As thou hast died for me,
Oh, may my love to thee
Pure, warm, and changeless be,
    A living fire.

While life's dark maze I tread,
And griefs around me spread,
    Be thou my guide—
Bid darkness turn to day,

Wipe sorrow's tears away,
Nor let me ever stray
  From thee aside.

When ends life's transient dream,
When death's cold sullen stream
  Shall o'er me roll,
Blest Saviour! then, in love,
Fear and distrust remove;
Oh, bear me safe above,
  A ransomed soul!

COURAGE TO LIVE

Grace Noll Crowell

1877-

I am the way, the truth, and the life.
  —John 14. 6.

To those who have tried and seemingly have failed,
Reach out, dear Lord, and comfort them today;
For those whose hope has dimmed, whose faith has paled,
Lift up some lighted heavenly torch, I pray.
They are so frightened, Lord; reach out a hand.
They are so hurt and helpless; be their friend.
Baffled and blind, they do not understand—
They think this dark and tangled road the end.

Oh, touch to flame their hope that has burned low,
And strike with fire faith's ashes that are dead.
Let them walk proudly once again, and go
Seeking the sure and steadfast light ahead.
Help them to move among their fellow men
With courage to live, courage to try again.

THE JEW TO JESUS
Florence Kiper Frank

And Pilate answered and said again unto them, What will ye then that I shall do unto him whom ye call the King of the Jews?
—*Mark 15-12*

O Man of my own people, I alone
Among these alien ones can know thy face,
I who have felt the kinship of thy race
Burn in me as I sit where they intone
Thy praises,—those who, striving to make known
A God for sacrifice, have missed the grace
Of thy sweet human meaning in its place,
Thou who art of our blood-bond and our own.

Are we not sharers of thy Passion? Yea,
In spirit-anguish closely by thy side
We have drained the bitter cup, and, tortured, felt
With thee the bruising of each heavy welt.
In every land is our Gethsemane.
A thousand times have we been crucified.

APPARITIONS
Thomas Curtis Clark
1877-

God grant us the last line.

Who goes there in the night,
   Across the storm-swept plain?
We are the ghosts of a valiant war—
   A million murdered men!

Who goes there, at the dawn,
   Across the sun-swept plain?
We are the hosts of those who swear:
   It shall not be again.

THE QUIET LIFE
Alexander Pope
1688-1744

Great is he who enjoys his earthenware as if it were plate, and not less great is the man to whom all his plate is no more than earthenware.—Leighton.

Happy the man, whose wish and care
A few paternal acres bound,
Content to breathe his native air
    In his own ground.

Whose herds with milk, whose fields with bread,
Whose flocks supply him with attire;
Whose trees in summer yield him shade,
    In winter, fire.

Blest, who can unconcern'dly find
Hours, days, and years, slide soft away
In health of body, peace of mind,
    Quiet by day,

Sound sleep by night; study and ease
Together mix'd; sweet recreation,
And innocence, which most does please
    With meditation.

Thus let me live, unseen, unknown;
Thus unlamented let me die;
Steal from the world, and not a stone
    Tell where I lie.

CIRCUMSTANCE
Alfred Tennyson
1809-1892

They do not heed the hurrying snow which covers
Their unremembered names,—Margaret and Joan,
Philip and Lucy, long forgotten lovers,—
Where the white silence of the drifts is blown.
—*Virginia Lyne Tunstall.*

Two children in two neighbor villages
Playing mad pranks along the healthy leas;
Two strangers meeting at a festival;
Two lovers whispering by an orchard wall;
Two lives bound fast in one with golden ease;
Two graves grass-green beside a gray church-tower,
Wash'd with still rains and daisy-blossomed;
Two children in one hamlet born and bred:
So runs the round of life from hour to hour.

AT JERUSALEM
Edna Dean Proctor
1825-1864

As the mountains are round about Jerusalem, so the Lord is round about his people from henceforth even forever.—Psalm 125, 2.

I stood by the Holy City
   Without the Damascus Gate,
While the wind blew soft from the distant sea,
   And the day was wearing late,
And swept its wide horizon
   With reverent lingering gaze
From the rolling uplands of the west
   That slope a hundred ways,

To Olivet's gray terraces
 By Kedron's bed that rise,
Upon whose crest the Crucified
 Was lost to mortal eyes;
And, far beyond, to the tawny line
 Where the sun seemed still to fall—
So bright the hue against the blue,
 Of Moab's mountain wall;
And north to the hills of Benjamin,
 Whose springs are flowing yet,
Ramah, and sacred Mizpah,
 Its dome above them set;
And the beautiful words of the Psalmist
 Had meaning before unknown:
As the hills are round Jerusalem
The Lord is round His own.

WITH WHOM IS NO VARIABLENESS

Arthur Hugh Clough

1819-1861

Every good and every perfect gift
 Is from above
And cometh down from the Father of lights,
With whom is no variableness
 Neither shadow of turning.
—James: 1, 17.

It fortifies my soul to know
That though I perish, truth is so;
That, howsoe'er I stray and range,
Whate'er I do, Thou dost not change.
I steadier step when I recall
That, if I slip, Thou dost not fall.

MARY AT THE CROSS
Clyde McGee

When every hill is made a Calvary! Whatever comfort the many mothers in how many lands may garner from our sympathy, it must console them to know that Mary, Mother, understands.

And Mary stood beside the cross! Her soul
Pierced with the self-same wound that rent His side
Who hung thereon. She watched Him, as He died.
Her son! Saw Him paying the cruel toll
Exacted by the law, and unbelief,
Since He their evil will had dared defy.
There stood the mother helpless in her grief,
Beside the cross, and saw her first-born die!

How many mothers in how many lands
Have bowed with Mary in her agony,
In silence borne the wrath of war's commands,
When every hill is made a Calvary!

O pity, Lord, these mothers of the slain,
And grant their dead shall not have died in vain.

GUIDANCE
Robert Browning
1812-1889

One step enough for me.—Cardinal Newman.

I see my way as birds their trackless way.
I shall arrive—what time, what circuit first,
I ask not; but
In some time, His good time, I shall arrive;
He guides me and the bird.

WE CALL THIS LIFE
Douglas Malloch
1877-

*And then the God that takes one small world
  from him
Gives him the skies.*

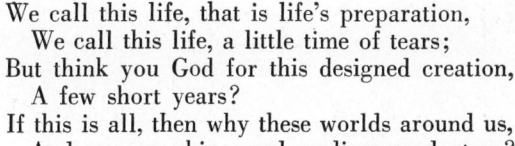

> We call this life, that is life's preparation,
>   We call this life, a little time of tears;
> But think you God for this designed creation,
>   A few short years?
> If this is all, then why these worlds around us,
>   And unseen skies, and undiscovered stars?
> I wonder, though one little world we found us,
>   Why God made Mars?
>
> A million spheres, and ours one tiny planet,
>   Eternity, and earth a little span—
> I cannot think for this that God began it,
>   That God made man.
> I eat, I drink, a little gold I win me,
>   One world enough for my necessities,
> But something else, some other thing within me,
>   Does none of these.
>
> My soul has little use for earthly treasure,
>   Comes not to table, wears no silk nor wool,
> With all our playthings, finds its only pleasure
>   The beautiful.
> So many things my soul has naught to do with,
>   To which the man of flesh so fondly clings;
> Shall that soul die with these things I am through with,
>   The fleshly things?
>
> God made for man an earthly habitation,
>   The body soil in which the soul may grow.
> This little life is but the preparation
>   The soul must know.

And then some day man's errors overcome him;
　　The body fails—the soul alone is wise;
And then the God that takes one small world from him
　　Gives him the skies.

O LOVE THAT LIGHTS THE EVENING SKY
Louis FitzGerald Benson
1855-1930

Though written in 1923, Dr. Benson's fine poem has been translated into all the great modern languages — into French for the Catholic cathedral of Lausanne, and into German Protestant church services. It was read at the author's funeral in October, 1930, and those present will never forget the profound emotion of that vast audience of his friends.

O Love that lights the eastern sky
　　And shrouds the evening rest,
From out whose hand the swallows fly,
　　Within whose heart they nest!

O life, content beneath the blue!
　　Or if, God will, the gray,
Then tranquil yet, till light breaks through
　　To melt the mist away.

O death that sails so close to shore
　　At twilight! From my gate
I scan the darkening sea once more,
　　And for its message wait.

What lies beyond the afterglow?
　　To life's new dawn how far?
As if an answer, spoken low,
　　Love lights the evening star.

HE LIVED A LIFE

H. N. Fifer

*All my life I have plucked a thistle
And planted a flower
Where I thought a flower would grow.*
—*Abraham Lincoln*

What was his creed?
I do not know his creed; I only know
That here below, he walked the common road
And lifted many a load, lightened the task,
Brightened the day for others toiling on a weary way:
This, his only meed; I do not know his creed.

What was his creed? I never heard him speak
Of visions rapturous, of Alpine peak
Of doctrine, dogma, new or old:
But this I know, he was forever bold
To stand alone, to face the challenge of each day,
And live the truth, so far as he could see—
The truth that evermore makes free.

His creed? I care not what his creed;
Enough that never yielded he to greed,
But served a brother in his daily need;
Plucked many a thorn and planted many a flower;
Glorified the service of each hour;
Had faith in God, himself, and fellow-men;
Perchance he never thought in terms of creed;
I only know he lived a life, in deed!

STRICKEN

Anonymous

What helm? Men hurry on—to what port? For what avails this eager pace? Better with John Burroughs—

> *Serene I fold my hands and wait,*
> *Nor care for wind, nor tide, nor sea;*
> *I rave no more 'gainst Time or Fate,*
> *For lo! my own shall come to me.*

His massive frame once held so proudly straight,
   Now sagged and drooped—a look of pained surprise
   Replacing former glance of friendly eyes;
"My memory's gone," he said, "my mental state
Confused, I must get well—duties await—
   Lord knows I'm needed at the helm," he sighs,
   As slowly dragging one poor foot, he plies
His labored way, unconscious of his fate.

To think that on a time this sorry wreck
   Had led in manly sports—this brilliant mind—
   This head—to nodding dullness now resigned,
In storm and stress held scores of men in check,
   And by its power enthralled and charmed mankind.
   Yet now forsaken, gropes, like one gone blind.

THE PRIMROSE PATH

William Shakspere

1564-1616

From Hamlet, 1, 3, 50.

> Do not, as some ungracious pastors do,
> Show me the steep and thorny way to heaven
> Whilst, like a puff'd and reckless libertine,
> Himself the primrose path of dalliance treads,
> And recks not his own rede.

THE CELESTIAL SURGEON
Robert Louis Stevenson
1850-1894

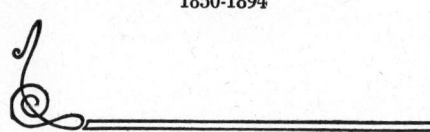

Stevenson, with small reason for physical happiness, left us a tradition of courage—a shining morning face, no matter what the night.

> If I have faltered more or less
> In my great task of happiness;
> If I have moved among my race
> And shown no shining morning face;
> If beams from happy human eyes
> Have moved me not; if morning skies,
> Books, and my food, and summer rain
> Knocked on my sullen heart in vain:—
> Lord, thy most pointed pleasure take
> And stab my spirit broad awake.

STILL, STILL WITH THEE
Harriet Beecher Stowe
1811-1896

Harriet Beecher Stowe, sister of the great Henry Ward Beecher, and author of Uncle Tom's Cabin, was an uncompromising foe of slavery. But she was more—a poet. This famous poem-song was set to the music of Mendelssohn, and is a permanent addition to sacred literature.

> Still, still with Thee, when purple morning breaketh,
>   When the bird waketh and the shadows flee;
> Fairer than morning, lovelier than the daylight,
>   Dawns the sweet consciousness, I am with Thee!
>
> Alone with Thee, amid the mystic shadows,
>   The solemn hush of nature newly born;
> Alone with Thee in breathless adoration,
>   In the calm dew and freshness of the morn.

When sinks the soul, subdued by toil, to slumber,
  Its closing eye looks up to Thee in prayer;
Sweet the repose beneath the wings o'er-shading,
  But sweeter still to wake and find Thee there.

So shall it be at last, in that bright morning
  When the soul waketh and life's shadows flee;
O in that hour, fairer than daylight dawning,
  Shall rise the glorious thought, I am with Thee!

HUSH, MY DEAR, LIE STILL AND SLUMBER
Isaac Watts
1674-1748

Like Pope, his contemporary, Watts was physically dwarfed and hopelessly weak and crippled. His father, a deacon in the Independent Church of Southampton had been imprisoned for religious non-conformity and his mother was wont to sit with little Isaac on the cold stone steps of the jail. But unlike Pope, his mind was not embittered by his twisted little body. One period of his life he gave to writing children's poems, the best of which is this little song known the world round.

Hush! my dear, lie still and slumber,
  Holy angels guard thy bed!
Heavenly blessings without number
  Gently falling on thy head.

Sleep, my babe; thy food and raiment,
  House and home, thy friends provide;
All without thy care or payment:
  All thy wants are well supplied.

How much better thou'rt attended
  Than the Son of Man could be,

When from heaven He descended
And became a child like thee!

Soft and easy is thy cradle,
Coarse and hard thy Saviour lay
When his birthplace was a stable
And his softest bed was hay.

ALONG THE ROAD
Robert Browning Hamilton

I walked a mile with Pleasure,
She chattered all the way,
But left me none the wiser
For all she had to say.

I walked a mile with Sorrow,
And ne'er a word said she;
But, oh, the things I learned from her
When Sorrow walked with me!

JOY, SHIPMATE, JOY
Walt Whitman
1819-1892

A widening heaven, a current without care.

Joy, shipmate, joy!
(Pleased to my soul at death I cry)
Our life is closed, our life begins,
The long, long anchorate we leave,
The ship is clear at last, she leaps!
She swiftly courses from the shore,
Joy, shipmate, joy!

THE OLD STOIC
Emily Brontë
1818-1848

Emily Brontë was a sister of Charlotte, author of the still famous novel, Jane Eyre. Born in a vicarage upon the desolate moors about Bradford, England, shut in, Charlotte, Emily, and Anne left broad names on the pages of British literature.
Emily, the best poet of them, was herself a stoic, enduring, deeply religious, wearing out against increasing family difficulties—but always self-reliant to the point of refusing a physician up to within an hour of her death.
Her poem is her autobiography.

Riches I hold in light esteem,
    And love I laugh to scorn;
And lust of fame was but a dream,
    That vanished with the morn:

And if I pray, the only prayer
    That moves my lips for me
Is, "Leave the heart that now I bear,
    And give me liberty!"

Yes, as my swift days near their goal,
    'Tis all that I implore;
In life and death a chainless soul,
    With courage to endure.

From THE UNIVERSAL PRAYER
Alexander Pope
1688-1744

Pope was a hopeless cripple. He could neither dress nor undress himself, and needed help in getting into or out of his bed. Yet he is, next to Shakspere, the most quoted poet of English.
Here is a great stanza from his Universal Prayer.

Teach me to feel another's woe,
    To hide the fault I see;
That mercy I to others show,
    That mercy show to me.

THE CHARIOT
Emily Dickinson
1830-1886

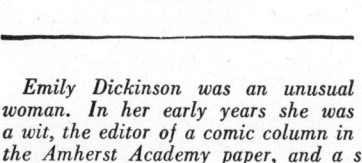

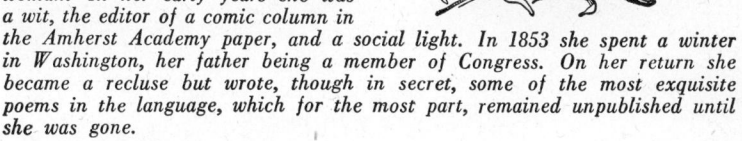

Emily Dickinson was an unusual woman. In her early years she was a wit, the editor of a comic column in the Amherst Academy paper, and a social light. In 1853 she spent a winter in Washington, her father being a member of Congress. On her return she became a recluse but wrote, though in secret, some of the most exquisite poems in the language, which for the most part, remained unpublished until she was gone.

> Because I could not stop for Death,
> He kindly stopped for me;
> The carriage held but just ourselves,
> And Immortality.
>
> We slowly drove, he knew no haste,
> And I had put away
> My labor and my leisure, too,
> For his civility.
>
> We passed the school where children played,
> Their lessons scarcely done;
> We passed the fields of grazing grain,
> We passed the setting sun.
>
> We paused before a house that seemed
> A swelling of the ground;
> The roof was scarcely visible,
> The cornice but a mound.
> Since then, 'tis centuries; but each
> Feels shorter than the day
> I first surmised the horses' heads
> Were toward eternity.

DIVINA COMMEDIA
Henry W. Longfellow
1807-1882

Longfellow recalls the great cathedrals of Europe that he knew and loved so well in this the first of a series of six sonnets to Dante.

Oft have I seen at some cathedral door
    A laborer, pausing in the dust and heat,
    Lay down his burden, and with reverent feet
Enter, and cross himself, and on the floor
Kneel to repeat his paternoster o'er;
    Far off noises of the world retreat;
    The loud vociferations of the street
Become an indistinguishable roar.
So, as I enter here from day to day,
    And leave my burden at this minster gate,
Kneeling in prayer, and not ashamed to pray,
    The tumult of the time disconsolate
To inarticulate murmurs dies away,
    While the eternal ages watch and wait.

THE JEWISH CONSCRIPT
Florence Kiper Frank

The World War brought Jew against Jew, everywhere.

They have dressed me up in a soldier's dress,
    With a rifle in my hand,
And have sent me bravely forth to shoot
    My own in a foreign land.

Many shall die for the fields of their homes,
    And many in conquest wild,
But I shall die for the fatherland
    That murdered my little child.

How many hundreds of years ago—
  The nations wax and cease!—
Did the God of our fathers doom us to bear
  The flaming message of peace!

We are the mock and the sport of time!
  Yet why should I complain!—
For a Jew that they hung on the bloody cross,
  He also died in vain.

BEYOND THE HORIZON

Robert Freeman

Robert Freeman, for more than a quarter of a century, pastor of the Pasadena Presbyterian Church, wrote Beyond the Horizon for his Easter services. It was first printed in the Christian Century and then in London papers, next in the Literary Digest, since when it has been a world-wide favorite.

When men go down to the sea in ships,
  'Tis not to the sea they go;
Some isle or pole the mariners' goal,
And thither they sail through calm and gale,
  When down to the sea they go.

When souls go down to the sea by ship,
  And the dark ship's name is Death,
Why mourn and wail at the vanishing sail?
Though outward bound, God's world is round,
  And only a ship is Death.

When I go down to the sea by ship,
  And Death unfurls her sail,
Weep not for me, for there will be
A living host on another coast
  To beckon and give "All Hail!"

IN THE GARDEN OF THE LORD
Helen Keller

Helen Keller, the most famous of our blind, was rendered dumb at an early age by the loss of both sight and hearing. But at seven, the famous Anna Mansfield Sullivan (Mrs. John A. Macy) came to her, with whose aid she was graduated with honors from Radcliffe. And then with the skilled help of Sarah Fuller she learned to speak. She is well known as a poet and an author, but most of all as one whose physical limitations could not limit the soul.

The word of God came unto me,
Sitting alone among the multitudes;
And my blind eyes were touched with light.
And there was laid upon my lips a flame of fire.

I laugh and shout, for life is good,
Though my feet are set in silent ways.
In merry mood I leave the crowd
To walk in my garden. Ever as I walk
I gather fruits and flowers in my hands.
And with joyful heart I bless the sun
That kindles all the place with radiant life.
I run with playful winds that blow the scent

Of rose and jessamine in eddying whirls.
At last I come where tall lilies grow,
Lifting their faces like white saints to God.
While the lilies pray, I kneel upon the ground;
I have strayed into the holy temple of the Lord.

HORACE
65-8 B. C.

Content with his past life—a goal for any life.

Content with his past life let him take leave of life like a satiated guest.

GOD OF OUR LIFE THROUGH ALL THE CIRCLING YEARS

Hugh T. Kerr

1871-

Written in 1916 on the occasion of the fiftieth-year celebration of the founding of the Shadyside Presbyterian Church, Pittsburgh.

God of our life, through all the circling years,
    We trust in Thee;
In all the past, through all our hopes and fears,
    Thy hand we see.
With each new day, when morning lifts the veil,
We own Thy mercies, Lord, which never fail.

God of the past, our times are in Thy hand;
    With us abide.
Lead us by faith to hope's true Promised Land;
    Be Thou our guide.
With Thee to bless, the darkness shines as light,
And faith's fair vision changes into sight.

God of the coming years, through paths unknown
    We follow Thee;
When we are strong, Lord, leave us not alone;
    Our Refuge be.
Be Thou for us in life our Daily Bread,
Our heart's true Home when all our years have sped.

PEACE
Clinton Scollard
1860-1932

Not with the high-voiced fife
    Nor with the deep-voiced drum,
To mark the end of strife
    The perfect peace shall come.

Nor pomp nor pageant grand
   Shall bring War's blest surcease,
But silent, from God's hand
   Shall come the perfect peace!

A PRAYER
Edwin Markham
1852-

The gentle Markham, dean of American poets, pleads for gentleness.

Teach me, Father, how to go
Softly as the grasses grow;
Hush my soul to meet the shock
Of the wild world as a rock;
But my spirit, propt with power,
Make as simple as a flower.
Let the dry heart fill its cup,
Like a poppy looking up;
Let life lightly wear her crown,
Like a poppy looking down.

Teach me, Father, how to be
Kind and patient as a tree.
Joyfully the crickets croon
Under shady oak at noon;
Beetle, on his mission bent,
Tarries in that cooling tent.
Let me, also, cheer a nook,
Place for friendly bread or book—
Place where passing souls can rest
On the way and be their best.

O LOVE, THAT WILT NOT LET ME GO

George Matheson

1842-1906

There is a popular belief that Matheson wrote O Love, That Wilt Not Let Me Go in solace of a love lost because he was going blind. It may even be so, for he did go blind, and the poem was written in June, 1882, on the evening of his sister's marriage. He says: "Something has happened to me, which was known only to myself, and which caused me the most severe mental suffering. ... I am quite sure the whole work was completed in five minutes and equally sure that it never received at my hand any retouching ..."

O Love, that wilt not let me go,
   I rest my weary soul on Thee;
I give Thee back the life I owe,
That in Thine ocean depths its flow
   May richer, fuller be.

O Light, that followest all my way,
   I yield my flickering torch to Thee;
My heart restores its borrowed ray,
That in Thy sunshine's blaze its day
   May brighter, fairer be.

O Joy, that seekest me through pain,
   I cannot close my heart to Thee;
I trace the rainbow through the rain,
And feel the promise is not vain,
   That morn shall tearless be.

O Cross, that liftest up my head,
   I dare not ask to fly from Thee;
I lay in dust life's glory dead,
And from the ground there blossoms red
   Life that shall endless be.

THE TOYS

Coventry Patmore

1823-1896

The elder Patmore (P. G.), father of Coventry, was associated with Lamb, Hazlett, "Barry Cornwall," and others; the son was an associate of Ruskin, Browning and Tennyson. The death of his wife in 1862 leaving him six small children qualifies him to speak for a child.

My little son, who looked from thoughtful eyes,
And moved and spoke in quiet grown-up wise,
Having my law the seventh time disobeyed,
I struck him, and dismissed,
With hard words and unkissed,
—His mother, who was patient, being dead.
Then, fearing lest his grief should hinder sleep,
I visited his bed,
But found him slumbering deep,
With darkened eyelids, and their lashes yet
From his late sobbing wet.
And I, with moan,
Kissing away his tears, left others of my own;
For, on a table drawn beside his head,
He had put, within his reach,
A box of counters and a red-veined stone,
A piece of glass abraded by the beach,
And six or seven shells,
A bottle with bluebells,
And two French copper coins, ranged there with careful art,
To comfort his sad heart.
So, when that night I prayed
To God, I wept, and said:

Ah, when at last we lie with trancèd breath,
Not vexing Thee in death,
And Thou rememberest of what toys
We made our joys,
How weakly understood
Thy great commanded good,
Then, fatherly not less
Than I whom Thou hast moulded from the clay,
Thou'lt leave Thy wrath, and say:
"I will be sorry for their childishness."

TO ONE SELF-SLAIN

Charles Hanson Towne

1877-

Shiftless and shy, gentle and kind and frail,
  Poor wanderer, bewildered into vice,
You are freed at last from seas you could not sail,
  A wreck upon the shores of Paradise.
              —*J. G. Squire, An Epitaph.*

When he went blundering back to God,
His songs half written, his work half done,
Who knows what paths his bruised feet trod,
What hills of peace or pain he won?

I hope God smiled and took his hand,
And said, "Poor truant, passionate fool!
Life's book is hard to understand;
Why could'st thou not remain at school?"

AN OLD WOMAN OF THE ROAD

Padraic Colum

1881-

More or less unique in the occidental world, are the wandering women of Ireland, resultants of a system of eviction. They are welcome in more fortunate homes, yet always homeless upon the roads and in the fields of their own land.

Oh, to have a little house!
To own the hearth and stool and all!
The heaped up sods upon the fire,
The pile of turf against the wall!

To have a clock with weights and chains
And pendulum swinging up and down!
A dresser filled with shining delph
Speckled and white and blue and brown!

I could be busy all the day
Clearing and sweeping hearth and floor,
And fixing on their shelf again
My white and blue and speckled store!

I could be quiet there at night
Beside the fire and by myself
Sure of a bed and loth to leave
The ticking clock and the shining delph!

Och! but I'm weary of mist and dark,
And roads where there's never a house nor bush,
And tired I am of bog and road,
And the crying wind and the lonesome hush!

And I am praying to God on high,
And I am praying Him night and day,
For a little house—a house of my own—
Out of the wind's and the rain's way.

"LET IT BE FORGOTTEN"

Sara Teasdale

1884-1934

One of the most beautiful phrases in the language—
Let it be forgotten . . .
. . . as a hushed footfall
In a long-forgotten snow.

Let it be forgotten, as a flower is forgotten,
   Forgotten as a fire that once was singing gold,
Let it be forgotten for ever and ever,
   Time is a kind friend, he will make us old.

If any one asks, say it was forgotten
   Long and long ago,
As a flower, as a fire, as a hushed footfall
   In a long-forgotten snow.

DEATH

Emily Dickinson

1830-1886

In spite of a meager output, Emily Dickinson has been called America's greatest woman poet. It was not until after her death that her work came prominently to the attention of lovers of poetry. She was unsurpassed in the art of giving an effective, even astounding turn to her closing phrase.

    The bustle in the house
    The morning after death
    Is solemnest of industries
    Enacted upon earth;—

    The sweeping up the heart
    And putting love away
    We shall not want to use again
    Until eternity.

EVENING HYMN

George Washington Doane
1799-1859

Bishop Doane was born the very year of the passing of the man for whom he was named, George Washington. And like Washington, he left ideals for succeeding generations. His Evening Hymn is one of the most beautiful in the language.

Softly now the light of day
Fades upon my sight away;
Free from care, from labor free,
Lord, I would commune with thee.

Thou, whose all-pervading eye
Naught escapes without, within,
Pardon each infirmity,
Open fault, and secret sin.

Soon, for me, the light of day
Shall forever pass away;
Then, from sin and sorrow free,
Take me, Lord, to dwell with thee.

Thou who, sinless, yet hast known,
All of man's infirmity;
Then from thine eternal throne,
Jesus, look with pitying eye.

CONSCIENCE
Nathaniel Hawthorne
1804-1864

And if thrice it is anesthesia.

If conscience smites thee once it is admonition; if twice it is condemnation.

LIFE

Sarojina Nayadu

1879-

Mrs. Nayadu is a Hindu woman. This searching poem, Life, appears in her first volume of poems, called The Golden Threshold.

Children, ye have not lived, to you it seems
Life is a lovely stalactite of dreams,
Or carnival of careless joys that leap
About your hearts like billows on the deep
In flames of amber and of amethyst.

Children, ye have not lived, ye but exist
Till some resistless hour shall rise and move
Your hearts to wake and hunger after love
And thirst with passionate longing for the things
That burn your brows with blood red sufferings.

Till ye have battled with great griefs and fears,
And borne the conflict of dream-shattering years,
Wounded with fierce desire and worn with strife,
Children, ye have not lived: for this is life.

KINSHIP

Angela Morgan

From Marcus Aurelius, Roman emperor in the second century after Christ: "The nature of the universe is the nature of things that are. Now things that are have kinship with things that are from the beginning."

I am aware
As I go commonly sweeping the stair
Doing my part of the every day care . . .

I am aware of the glory that runs
From the core of myself to the core of the suns.

Bound to the stars by invisible chains,
Blaze of eternity now in my veins,
Seeing the rush of ethereal rains
Here in the midst of the everyday air—
I am aware.

I am aware,
As I sit quietly here in my chair,
Sewing or reading or braiding my hair—
Human and simple my lot and my share . .

I am aware of the splendor that ties
All the things of the earth with the things of the skies,
Here in my body the heavenly heat,
Here in my flesh the melodious beat
Of the planets that circle Divinity's feet.
As I sit silently here in my chair
I am aware.

THE TEARS OF MARY

Theodosia Garrison

The conflict of mother love and divine love in the heart of Mary has long been the subject of thought and emotion. There is another great poem elsewhere in this volume, that treats of Mother and Son, Agnes Lee's The Christ Child.

"Nay, but He is so helpless and so sweet,
Why, it is nothing more than if I pressed
An armful of white roses to my breast,
That only stir above my own heart's beat.
Why should a dream I dreamed destroy my rest?"
Yet even as she spake she felt the stir
Of wings that in the garden passed by her.

*"He is so small, so weak against my heart,
A little wounded dove were strong as He.
He hath no other need than of me,
Nor any life from my own life apart.
Why should I dread an olden prophecy?"*
Yet even as she spake, she felt, like flame,
The voice that in the garden said her name.

*"As lesser mothers are, am I not blest?
He is no other's but mine own, mine own,
No King, no Prophet, but my child alone.
Asking no other kingdom than my breast.
Let me be glad those foolish fears are done."*
Yet even as she spake He stirred in her embrace,
Feeling her tears, her tears—upon His face.

WORSHIP

Helen Welshimer

God is a circle whose center is everywhere, and its circumference nowhere.
—Empedocles, Greek Philosopher, about 500 B.C.

I went to church—
An organ played;
Candles marched in white parade
On the altar;
Through stained glass
I saw the King of Battles pass.
Half afraid, I could not say
"My Father" in a quiet way.

And I who know
A simple God
Who puts brown seeds in rain-wet sod
And stoops to hear
A small child's rhyme
Come up in prayer at candle-time,
Did not find the God I knew,
Though I knelt and wanted to.

I went up a windy hill,
When the dusk was blue and still,
And sat awhile,
And watched a star . . .
Heaven wasn't very far.
I sang no songs,
I made no prayer—
I think God saw me sitting there.

IDENTITY
Thomas Bailey Aldrich
1836-1907

*It was evening here
But upon earth the very noon of night.
—Dante, Purgatorius.*

Somewhere—in desolate wind-swept space—
In Twilight-land—in No-man's land—
Two hurrying Shapes met face to face,
　And bade each other stand.

"And who are you?" cried one, agape,
Shuddering in the gleaming light.
"I know not," said the second Shape,
　"I only died last night."

FAITH AND HOPE
Sir Robert Grant
1779-1838

Sir Robert Grant was of a famous family, the son of a member of Parliament, and a director of the famous East India Company. Robert himself became governor of Bombay, and privy counselor. The Grants were known for their humanity, especially for their opposition to slavery.

To all of us, at times, days are dark and friends are few.

When gathering clouds around I view,
And days are dark, and friends are few
On him I lean, who, not in vain,
Experienced every human pain;
He sees my wants, allays my fears,
And counts and treasures up my tears.

If aught should tempt my soul to stray
From heavenly virtue's narrow way—
To fly the good I would pursue,
Or do the sin I would not do—
Still he, who felt temptation's power
Shall guard me in that dangerous hour.

When sorrowing o'er some stone, I bend,
Which covers all that was a friend,
And from his voice, his hand, his smile,
Divides me, for a little while,
My Saviour sees the tears I shed,
For Jesus wept o'er Lazarus dead.

And, if, when I have safely passed
Through every conflict but the last—
Still, still unchanging, watch beside
My painful bed—for thou hast died;
Then point to realms of cloudless day,
And wipe my latest tear away.

THE COTTER'S SATURDAY NIGHT

Robert Burns

1759-1796

Burns had made his songs for a brief ten years. He had written no epic and all his verse was in a dialect strange to English readers. Yet he died leaving poetry a different thing from what it had been when he found it.

To some extent, this was because he took poetry away from fine houses and fine people. Gray in his famous "Elegy" had got as far as writing about humble folk who had been safely laid beneath their tombstones. Burns wrote about them as they lived. In "The Cotter's Saturday Night" he describes a simple peasant family, drawing from his own father the picture of a farmer returning after his day's toil.—Joseph Auslander in The Winged Horse.

November chill blaws loud wi' angry sugh;
   The short'ning winter-day is near a close;
The miry beasts retreating frae the pleugh,
   The black'ning trains o' craws to their repose:
   The toil-worn cotter frae his labor goes,—
This night his weekly moil is at an end,—
   Collects his spades, his mattocks, and his hoes,
Hoping the morn in ease and rest to spend,
And weary, o'er the moor, his course does hameward bend.

At length his lonely cot appears in view,
   Beneath the shelter of an aged tree;
Th' expectant wee things, toddlin', stacher through
   To meet their dad, wi' flichterin' noise and glee.
   His wee bit ingle, blinking bonnily,
His clean hearthstane, his thriftie wifie's smile,
   The lisping infant prattling on his knee,
Does a' his weary carking cares beguile,
And makes him quite forget his labor and his toil.

Belyve, the elder bairns come drapping in,
   At service out, amang the farmers roun':
Some ca' the pleugh, some herd, some tentie rin
   A cannie errand to a neebor town;
   Their eldest hope, their Jenny, woman grown,
In youthfu' bloom, love sparkling in her e'e,
   Comes hame, perhaps to shew a braw new gown,
Or deposit her sair-won penny-fee,
To help her parents dear, if they in hardship be.

With joy unfeigned, brothers and sisters meet,
   And each for other's weelfare kindly spiers:
The social hours, swift-winged, unnoticed fleet;
   Each tells the uncos that he sees or hears;
   The parents, partial, eye their hopeful years;
Anticipation forward points the view.
   The mother, wi' her needle and her shears,
Gars auld claes look amaist as weel's the new —
The father mixes a' wi' admonition due.

Their master's and their mistress's command,
   The younkers a' are warnèd to obey;
And mind their labors wi' an eydent hand,
   And ne'er, though out o' sight, to jauk or play:
   "And oh! be sure to fear the Lord alway!
And mind your duty, duly, morn and night!
   Lest in temptation's path ye gang astray,
Implore His counsel and assisting might:
They never sought in vain that sought the Lord aright!"

But, hark! a rap comes gently to the door;
   Jenny, who kens the meaning o' the same,
Tells how a neebor lad cam o'er the moor,
   To do some errands, and convoy her hame.
   The wily mother sees the conscious flame
Sparkle in Jenny's e'e, and flush her cheek;
   Wi' heart-struck anxious care inquires his name,
While Jenny hafflins is afraid to speak;
Weel pleased the mother hears it's nae wild, worthless rake.

Wi' kindly welcome, Jenny brings him ben;
   A strappin' youth; he taks the mother's eye;
Blithe Jenny sees the visit's no ill-ta'en;
   The father cracks of horses, pleughs, and kye.
The youngster's artless heart o'erflows wi' joy,
   But blate and laithfu', scarce can weel behave;
   The mother, wi' a woman's wiles, can spy
What makes the youth sae bashfu' and sae grave;
Weel pleased to think her bairn's respected like the lave.

Oh, happy love! where love like this is found!
   Oh, heartfelt raptures! bliss beyond compare!
I've pacèd much this weary, mortal round,
   And sage experience bids me this declare:—
   If Heaven a draught of heavenly pleasure spare,
One cordial in this melancholy vale,
   'Tis when a youthful, loving, modest pair
In other's arms breathe out the tender tale,
Beneath the milk-white thorn that scents the evening gale.

But now the supper crowns their simple board,—
   The healsome parritch, chief o' Scotia's food;
The soupe their only hawkie does afford,
   That 'yont the hallan snugly chows her cood:
   The dame brings forth, in complimental mood,
To grace the lad, her weel-hain'd kebbuck, fell,
   And aft he's prest, and aft he ca's it guid;
The frugal wifie, garrulous, will tell,
How 't was a towmont auld, sin' lint was i' the bell.

The cheerfu' supper done, wi' serious face,
   They, round the ingle, form a circle wide;
The sire turns o'er, with patriarchal grace,
   The big ha' Bible, ance his father's pride;
   His bonnet rev'rently is laid aside,
His lyart haffets wearing thin and bare;
   Those strains that once did sweet in Zion glide,
He wales a portion with judicious care,
And "Let us worship God!" he says, with solemn air.

The priest-like father reads the sacred page—
　How Abram was the friend of God on high;
Or Moses bade eternal warfare wage
　With Amalek's ungracious progeny;
　Or how the royal bard did groaning lie
Beneath the stroke of Heaven's avenging ire;
　Or Job's pathetic plaint, and wailing cry;
　Or rapt Isaiah's wild, seraphic fire;
Or other holy seers that tune the sacred lyre.

Perhaps the Christian volume is the theme—
　How guiltless blood for guilty man was shed:
How He, who bore in heaven the second name,
　Had not on earth whereon to lay His head;
　How His first followers and servants sped;
The precepts sage they wrote to many a land:
　How he, who lone in Patmos banishèd,
Saw in the sun a mighty angel stand,
And heard great Bab'lon's doom pronounced by Heaven's command.

Then kneeling down, to Heaven's Eternal King,
　The saint, the father, and the husband prays:
Hope "springs exulting on triumphant wing,"
　That thus they all shall meet in future days:
　There ever bask in uncreated rays,
No more to sigh, or shed the bitter tear,
　Together hymning their Creator's praise,
　In such society, yet still more dear;
While circling Time moves round in an eternal sphere.

Compared with this, how poor Religion's pride,
　In all the pomp of method and of art,
When men display to congregations wide
　Devotion's every grace, except the heart!
　The Power, incensed, the pageant will desert,
The pompous strain, the sacerdotal stole;
　But haply, in some cottage far apart,
May hear, well pleased, the language of the soul;
And in His book of life the inmates poor enrol.

Then homeward all take off their several way;
  The youngling cottagers retire to rest:
The parent-pair their secret homage pay,
  And proffer up to Heaven the warm request,
  That He who stills the raven's clamorous nest,
And decks the lily fair in flowery pride,
  Would, in the way His wisdom sees the best,
For them and for their little ones provide;
But chiefly, in their hearts with grace divine preside.

From scenes like these old Scotia's grandeur springs,
  That makes her loved at home, revered abroad:
Princes and lords are but the breath of kings,
  "An honest man's the noblest work of God;"
  And certes, in fair Virtue's heavenly road,
The cottage leaves the palace far behind:
  What is a lordling's pomp?—a cumbrous load,
Disguising oft the wretch of human kind,
Studied in arts of hell, in wickedness refined!

O Scotia! my dear, my native soil!
  For whom my warmest wish to Heaven is sent,
Long may thy hardy sons of rustic toil
  Be blest with health, and peace, and sweet content!
  And oh! may Heaven their simple lives prevent
From luxury's contagion, weak and vile!
  Then, howe'er crowns and coronets be rent,
A virtuous populace may rise the while,
And stand a wall of fire around their much-loved isle.

O Thou! who poured the patriotic tide,
  That streamed through Wallace's undaunted heart,
Who dared to nobly stem tyrannic pride,
  Or nobly die, the second glorious part,
  (The patriot's God, peculiarly Thou art,
His friend, inspirer, guardian, and reward!)
  O never, never, Scotia's realm desert;
But still the patriot, and the patriot-bard
In bright succession raise, her ornament and guard!

AUREOLE
Helene Magaret

*Who seeks for heaven alone to save his soul,
May keep the faith, but will not reach the goal.*
—*Henry van Dyke.*

I once praised loneliness and said:
In this way only shall I grow,
By walking fields no others tread,
By finding lakes no others know.

Deep in my heart I prayed the years
Should grant my spirit be renewed
As Francis' was, in faith and tears,
And self-immuring solitude.

I did not know that those who walk
From year to year, dear Love, alone
Often grow bold-eyed like the hawk
Or undiscerning like the stone.

Now to my peace I understand
That none may reach the heaven's height
Unless he go there hand in hand
With one who likewise covets light.

THE DIFFERENCE
John Bannister Tabb
1845-1909

John Bannister Tabb was a captain's mate on a blockade runner in the Civil War; then a Catholic priest; and until he went blind, an instructor in English literature in St. Charles College, where he established his fame as a poet.

Unc' Si, de Holy Bible say,
  In speakin' of de jus',
Dat he do fall seben times a day;
  Now, how's de sinner wuss?

"Well, chile, de slip may come to all,
  But den de diff'ence foller;
For, ef you watch him when he fall,
  De jus' man do not waller."

PROVIDENCE
William Cowper
1731-1800

Like Addison, Cowper's fame is literary rather than religious. His ballad John Gilpin is widely known, and his translation of Homer one of the best in the language. His shorter poems are in every anthology.

And like Pope and Watts, he was ill of body and, at times, unsound of mind. Sensitive, introspective, he was unable to finish out his education at Westminster school, attempting suicide rather than appear in public examination. Yet from his gifted pen have come some of the great inspirational lines of religious literature.

God moves in a mysterious way
  His wonders to perform;
He plants his footsteps in the sea,
  And rides upon the storm.

* * * * *

Ye fearful saints, fresh courage take!
  The clouds ye so much dread
Are big with mercy, and will break
  In blessings on your head.

Judge not the Lord by feeble sense,
  But trust him for his grace;
Behind a frowning providence
  He hides a smiling face.

His purposes will ripen fast,
  Unfolding every hour;
The bud may have a bitter taste,
  But sweet will be the flower.

Blind unbelief is sure to err,
   And scan his work in vain;
God is his own interpreter,
   And he will make it plain.

WHO LOVES THE RAIN
Frances Shaw

For what avails this eager pace?

Who loves the rain,
   And loves his home,
And looks on life with quiet eyes,
   Him will I follow through the storm;
   And at his hearth-fire keep me warm;
Nor hell nor heaven shall that soul surprise,
   Who loves the rain,
   And loves his home,
And looks on life with quiet eyes.

STAY, STAY AT HOME, MY HEART, AND REST
Henry W. Longfellow
1807-1882

He is happiest, be he king or peasant, who finds peace in his home.—Goethe.

Stay, stay at home, my heart, and rest;
Home-keeping hearts are happiest,
For those that wander they know not where
Are full of trouble and full of care;
   To stay at home is best.

Weary and homesick and distressed,
They wander east, they wander west,
And are baffled and beaten and blown about
By the winds of the wilderness of doubt;
　To stay at home is best.

CHRIST OF THE ANDES

Florence Earle Coates

1850-1927

High in the snowy Andes on the border between Argentina and Chile, stands the mighty statue, The Christ of the Andes. There was once strife as to the boundary, but Bishop Benavente of Argentina, and Bishop Java of Chile, collaborated to set up a great Christ, cast from melted cannon, on the side of which is the legend:
　"Sooner shall these mountains crumble into dust than the people of Argentina and Chile break the peace which they have sworn to maintain at the feet of Christ the Redeemer."
　A reproduction of The Christ of the Andes stands in the Peace Palace in The Hague.

Far, far the mountain peak from me
Where lone he stands, with look caressing;
　Yet from the valley, wistfully
　I lift my dreaming eyes, and see
His hand stretched forth in blessing.

Never bird sings nor blossom blows
Upon the summit chill and breathless
　Where throned he waits amid the snows;
　But from his presence wide outflows
Love that is warm and deathless!

O Symbol of the great release
From war and strife!—unfailing fountain
　To which we turn for joy's increase,
　Fain would we climb to heights of Peace—
Thy peace upon the mountain!

HE PRAYETH BEST
Samuel Taylor Coleridge
1772-1834

These are some of the closing stanzas of Coleridge's famous Ancient Mariner. The old grey-beard had stopped the wedding guest and held him with skinny hand and glittering eye long past the wedding hour, while he poured into his ear the tale of a ship that sailed to the far frigid south, round land, and back north again, and the terrible things that befell him because of his guilty slaying of the friendly albatross. At length, the tale being done, he releases the Wedding-Guest:

O Wedding-Guest! this soul hath been
  Alone on a wide, wide sea:
So lonely 'twas, that God Himself
  Scarce seemèd there to be.

O sweeter than the marriage-feast,
  'Tis sweeter far to me
To walk together to the kirk
  With a goodly company!—

To walk together to the kirk
  And all together pray,
While each to his great Father bends,
Old men, and babes, and loving friends,
  And youths, and maidens gay.

Farewell, farewell! but this I tell
  To thee, thou Wedding-Guest!
He prayeth well who loveth well,
  Both man and bird and beast.

He prayeth best who loveth best,
    All things both great and small:
For the dear God, who loveth us,
    He made and loveth all.

BARABBAS
William E. Brooks
1875-

Jesus had been arrested by the Roman soldiers and dragged before Annas, the High Priest. Annas sent Him before Caiaphas, who sent Him to Pilate.

But ye have a custom, that I should release unto you one at the passover: will ye therefore that I release unto you the King of the Jews?

Then cried they all again, saying, Not this man, but Barabbas. Now Barabbas was a robber.—John 18:39, 40.

Barabbas speaks:

By what strange whimsies is a man's fate swayed,
I free to go, while he goes to his cross!
I know his life, no evil has he done,
For many a day in towns of Galilee
Have I stood in that crowd that swarmed him round
While his fingers healed the leper with their touch
Or at his word the devils fled away.
And men know my life, all my evil fame—
Now I stand free while he goes there to die!
What was there to this man that Annas feared,
And that dull Roman with his oily face?
He would be king? Nay, rather he would not!

Such men as he would never bind with crowns
And all the stiff seclusion of a throne
Their right to mix with men. Some deeper thought
Lay in that false priest's brain. Could it have been
He feared the words he spake about High God,
About men grown to stature of God's sons,
One brotherhood that banished self from earth?
No priest could gull a race that held such thoughts,
Nor was there place for Pilate in such plan,
Nor for Barabbas! No wonder Annas feared
A world he could not mold for his own gain.
And does he think to end him with a Cross?

WISDOM

The Bible

Proverbs 3, 16-17.

    Length of days is in her right hand;
      And in her left hand
    Riches and honour.

    Her ways are ways of pleasantness
      And all her paths
    Are peace.

CAMPUS
Margaret Sangster

*Time flies? Nay, time stays; we go.
This Margaret Sangster is the granddaughter of the other Margaret Sangster.*

The creeping ivy clings against gray towers,
The trees are old and wise and very tall,
Their shadows lie, like lace, on every wall,
A mellow clock chimes out the drifting hours,
As if to say, "Time slips, while learning flowers—
So many feet have echoed through each hall,
So many years have gone beyond recall,
So many sun-swept days, so many showers."

Perhaps these gray stones, robed in ivy, feel
That students strolling past are but a dream.
Perhaps the boys and girls with youth agleam
Are phantom-like and just a bit unreal
To the tall trees that, standing calmly by,
Draw strength and knowledge from the far-flung sky.

COME
Anna Letitia Barbauld
1743-1825

Mrs. Barbauld will always be remembered for her beautiful poem, Life.

Come, said Jesus' sacred voice,
Come, and make My paths your choice;
I will guide you to your home,
Weary pilgrim, hither come!

Thou who, houseless, sole, forlorn,
Long hast borne the proud world's scorn,

Long hast roamed the barren waste,
Weary pilgrim, hither haste.

Ye who, tossed on beds of pain,
Seek for ease, but seek in vain;
Ye, by fiercer anguish torn,
In remorse for guilt who mourn;

Hither come! for here is found
Balm that flows for every wound,
Peace that ever shall endure,
Rest eternal, sacred, sure.

THE MOTHERS OF MEN
Joaquin Miller
1841-1913

I think it must somewhere be written, that the virtues of mothers shall be visited on their children, as well as the sins of the fathers.—Dickens.

The bravest battle that ever was fought;
   Shall I tell you where and when?
On the maps of the world you will find it not,
   'Twas fought by the mothers of men.

Nay, not with cannon or battle shot,
   With sword or braver pen,
Nay, not with eloquent word or thought,
   From mouths of wonderful men;

But deep in a woman's walled-up heart,
   Of woman that would not yield,
But patiently, silently bore her part,—
   Lo, there is that battlefield.

No marshaling troops, no bivouac song;
  No banner to gleam and wave;
But, O those battles, they last so long,
  From babyhood to the grave!

Yet faithful still as a bridge of stars,
  She fights in her walled-up town
Fights on and on in the endless wars,
  Then silent, unseen, goes down.

THE MAN, CHRIST

Theresa Lindsey

The life He lived has never been assailed,
Nor any precept, as He lived it, yet
Has ever failed.

He built no temple, yet the farthest sea
Can yield no shore that's barren of His place
For bended knee.

He wrote no book and yet His words and prayer
Are intimate on many myriad tongues
And counsel everywhere.

He left no wealth yet year by year there came
Accumulated beauty of the world
To bear His name.

He never sought life's meaning to expound;
He simply quickened it by faith in God
Abysmally profound.

What artless witness is this world to be
Content to reckon every rising sun
From His nativity!

MY OWN SONG

Harriet Prescott Spofford

1835-1921

I were but little happy if I could say how much.
—Shakspere.

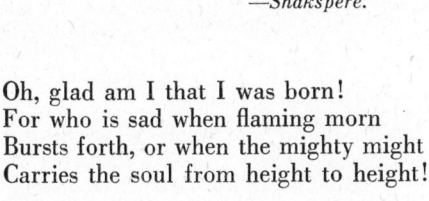

Oh, glad am I that I was born!
For who is sad when flaming morn
Bursts forth, or when the mighty might
Carries the soul from height to height!

To me, as to the child that sings,
The bird that claps his rain-washed wings,
The breeze that curls the sun-tipped flower,
Comes some new joy with each new hour.

Joy in the beauty of the earth,
Joy in the fire upon the hearth,
Joy in that potency of love
In which I live and breathe and move!

Joy even in the shapeless thought
That, some day, when all tasks are wrought,
I shall explore that vasty deep
Beyond the frozen gates of sleep.

For joy attunes all beating things,
With me each rythmic atom sings,
From glow till gloom, from mirk till morn;
Oh, I am glad that I was born!

THE LAST WORD
Matthew Arnold
1822-1888

*Cowards may fear to die; but courage stout,
Rather than live in snuff will be put out.*
—*Sir Walter Raleigh, on the night before his execution.*

Creep into thy narrow bed,
Creep, and let no more be said!
Vain thy onset! all stands fast.
Thy thyself must break at last.

Let the long contention cease!
Geese are swans, and swans are geese.
Let them have it how they will!
Thou art tired; best be still.

They out-talked thee, hissed thee, tore thee?
Better men fared thus before thee;
Fired their ringing shot and passed,
Hotly charged—and sank at last.

Charge once more, then, and be dumb!
Let the victors, when they come,
When the forts of folly fall,
Find thy body by the wall.

SPEAK GENTLY
David Bates

Good God! why should they mock poor fellows thus?—Shakspere.

Speak gently, kindly, to the poor;
  Let no harsh term be heard;
They have enough they must endure
  Without an unkind word

A SONG OF LIVING
William Stanley Braithwaite
1878-

Mr. Braithwaite is the editor of almost twenty annual volumes of current poetry. Many writers who have gone on to fame owe their start to this dean of anthologists.

> *My worthy friend, gray all our theories,*
> *And green alone, Life's golden tree.*
> —Goethe, Faust.

It is so good to be alive:
To have deep dreams: to greatly strive
Through the day's work: to dance and sing
Between the times of sorrowing—
To have a clear faith in the end
That death is life's best, truthful friend.

To be alive: to hear and see
This wonderful, strange pageantry
Of earth, in which each hour's session
Brings forth a new unknown procession
Of joys: stars, flowers, seas and grass
In ever new guise before me pass.

To have deep dreams: ah me, ah me!
To bring far things close by to see;
To have my voyaging soul explore
Beyond my body's ponderous door.
To make my love from a thousand graces,
Seen in a thousand women's faces.

To greatly strive: perform my share
Of work: for the world grows more fair
To him who measures Time and Fate
By what his laboring days create—
For work is the voice that lifts to God
The adoration of the sod.

To dance and sing: my body's praise
For being fair in many ways.
It hath no other voice than this
To thank God for a moment's bliss—
When art and heaven together trust
Joy to the perfection of the dust.

Times of sorrowing: yea, to weep:
To wash my soul with tears, and keep
It clean from earth's too constant gain,
Even as a flower needs the rain
To cool the passion of the sun,
And take a fresh new glory on.

To have clear faith:—through good or ill
We but perform some conscious will
Higher than man's. The world at best
In all things doth but manifest
That God has set His eternal seal
Upon the unsubstantial real.

THE PLEDGE OF CHEERFULNESS

William Cowper
1731-1800

*As fast locked up in sleep
As guiltless labor.*
—Shakspere.

Absence of occupation is not rest,
A mind quite vacant is a mind distress'd.
Come hither, ye that press your beds of down
And sleep not: see him sweating o'er his bread
Before he eats it:—'Tis the primal curse,
But soften'd into mercy; made the pledge
Of cheerful days, and nights without a groan.

ART THOU WEARY
John Mason Neale
1818-1866

John Mason Neale was a noted classical scholar, having won many honors in Trinity College, Cambridge. He chose a lowly life of service in Sackville College, East Grimstead, an obscure almshouse, and there passed his life.

His translation of a poem by St. Stephen of Mars Saba is very beautiful.

Art thou weary, art thou languid,
   Art thou sore distressed?
"Come to me," said One, "and coming,
   Be at rest."

Hath he marks to lead me to him,
   If he be my Guide?—
"In his feet and hands are wound-prints,
   And his side."

* * * * *

If I find him, if I follow,
   What his guerdon here?—
"Many a sorrow, many a labor,
   Many a tear."

If I still hold closely to him,
   What hath he at last?—
"Sorrow vanquished, labor ended,
   Jordan passed."

If I ask him to receive me,
   Will he say me nay?—
"Not till earth, and not till heaven
   Pass away."

* * * * *

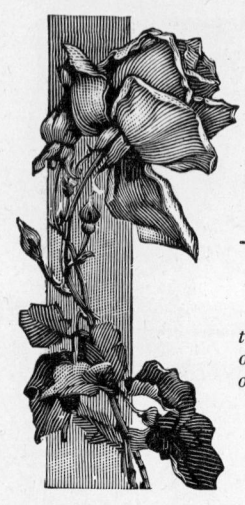

THE WAYS OF DEATH
William Ernest Henley
1849-1903

While yet a boy, William Ernest Henley contracted tuberculosis of the bones, necessitating the amputation of a foot, and months of illness. Yet he is the author of Invictus—

> *It matters not how strait the gate,*
> *How charged with punishments the scroll,*
> *I am the master of my fate;*
> *I am the captain of my soul.*

The menace of the years found him unafraid, the joy of living burst out in lyrics like The Blackbird (with his box-wood flute), and Sundown was fair. (So Be My Passing)

> *. . . and in my heart,*
> *Some late lark singing,*
> *Let me be gather'd to the quiet west,*
> *The sundown, splendid and serene,*
> *Death.*

The ways of Death are soothing and serene,
And all the words of Death are grave and sweet,
From camp and church, the fireside and the street,
She signs to come, and strife and song have been.

The summer night descending cool and green
And dark, on daytime's dust and stress and heat,
The ways of Death are soothing and serene,
And all the words of Death are grave and sweet.

O glad and sorrowful, with triumphant mien
And hopeful faces look upon and greet
This last of all your lovers and to meet
Her kiss, the Comforter's, your spirit lean—
The ways of Death are soothing and serene.

THE CRISIS
Ethelyn Bryant Chapman

Mrs. Chapman wrote The Crisis from a hospital room in Chicago. We who have tossed through the hot and shifting cinema of fevered psychosis will readily recognize its fidelity.

An Evil Eye, the tiny night-bulb glowed
Set in the blankness of the high gray walls
That prisoned pain. A ghostly-footed nurse
Moved in a shadow down the corridor.

"Hold fast tonight what we have gained," you said,
And speaking, placed in my reluctant hands
The reins that held those plunging ebon steeds,
The untamed leaders of an outlaw herd.
Your gray smile was a moonbeam in the room,
Then . . . dark closed round; grim cañons hemmed me in.

Along thin ledges, brittle with death's frost,
Those screaming stallions tore against the wind;
Across frail bridges, spider-webbed above,
Torrential rivers roaring far below,
Thundered the flailing of unmetaled hoofs,
And where the road's end jutted into air
Around some sudden bend, an icy blast
Flung back to blind my sight, thick-lathered sweat.

When the reins slackened in my tortured palms
I heard the sternly-kind command, "Hold fast!"
So, through the ghastly perils of that night
I brought those wild things, gentled and dull-eyed,
To the tame safety of corralling gates.

THE OLD AMATI
Oliver Wendell Holmes
1809-1894

Not infrequently the singing prose of master writers is found truly to be poetry. This is from the prose of "The Autocrat of the Breakfast Table"; and doubtless Holmes never thought of it as a poem.

Violins, too,—
The sweet old Amati!—
The mellow Stradivarius!
Played on by ancient *maestros*
Until the bow-hand lost its power
And the flying fingers stiffened.

Bequeathed to the passionate young enthusiast
Who made it whisper his hidden love,
And cry his inarticulate longings,
And scream his untold agonies,
And wail his monotonous despair.

Passed from his dying hand to the cold *virtuoso*
Who let it slumber in its case for a generation
Till
When his hord was broken up,
It came forth once more,
And rode the stormy symphonies of royal orchestras
Beneath the rushing bow of their lord and master.

Into lonely prisons with improvident artists;
Into convents from which arose, day and night,
The holy hymns with which its tones were blended;

And back again to orgies in which
It learned to howl and laugh
As if a legion of devils were shut up in it.

Then again to the gentle *dilettante*
Who calmed it down with easy melodies
Until it answered him softly
As in the days of the old *maestros*.

And so given into our hands,
Its pores full of music;
Stained, like the meerschaum, through and through
With the concentrated hue of all the harmonies
That have kindled and faded on its strings.

GOD MAKES A PATH
Roger Williams
1604?-1684

This is the same Roger Williams whose plea for general religious toleration, and for fair play for the Indians, brought his banishment from the Massachusetts colonies. God made him a path in the pathless wilderness until, in 1636, he was able to found Rhode Island.

God makes a path, provides a guide,
  And feeds in wilderness!
His glorious name while breath remains,
  O that I may confess.

Lost many a time, I have had no guide,
  No house, but hollow tree!
In stormy winter night no fire,
  No food, no company:

In him I found a house, a bed,
  A table, company:
No cup so bitter, but's made sweet,
  When God shall sweetening be.

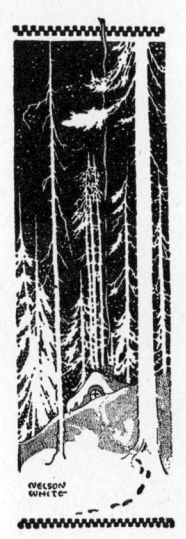

THE OLD MAN'S MOTTO

John Godfrey Saxe
1816-1887

*To grim despair be not a prey;
Bethink thee, "This will pass away."*

"Give me a motto," said a youth
  To one whom years had rendered wise;
"Some pleasant thought, or weighty truth,
  That briefest syllables comprise;
Some word of warning or of cheer
To grave upon my signet here.

"And, reverend father," said the boy,
  "Since life, they say, is ever made
A mingled web of grief and joy;
  Since cares may come and pleasures fade,—
Pray, let the motto have a range
Of meaning matching every change."

"Sooth!" said the sire, "methinks you ask
  A labor something over-nice,
That well a finer brain might task.
  What think you, lad, of this device
(Older than I, though I am gray).
'Tis simple,—'This will pass away.'

When wafted on by fortune's breeze,
  In endless peace thou seem'st to glide,
Prepare betimes for rougher seas,
  And check the boast of foolish pride;
Though smiling joy is thine today,
Remember, 'This will pass away.'

When all the sky is draped in black.
And, beaten by tempestuous gales,
Thy shuddering ship seems all a-wrack,
Then trim again thy tattered sails;
To grim despair be not a prey;
Bethink thee, 'This will pass away.'

Thus, O my son, be not o'er-proud,
Nor yet cast down; judge thou aright;
When skies are clear, expect the cloud;
In darkness wait the coming light;
Whatever be thy fate today,
Remember, 'This will pass away.' "

HUDIBRAS

Samuel Butler

1612-1680

Hudibras, the most extensive and devastating satire in English was written against the excesses of the Puritans in the England of Cromwell. It is natural that a political poem of the type should have been immensely popular with the lords and ladies of the Restoration; but it contains lines like the following that are significant beyond political setting, tho they are poor religion.

He was of that stubborn crew
Of errant saints, whom all men grant
To be the true church militant;
Such as do build their faith upon
The holy text of pike and gun;
Decide all controversies by
Infallible artillery,
And prove their doctrines orthodox
By apostolic blows and knocks;
Call fire, and sword, and desolation
A Godly, thorough Reformation,
Which always must be carried on
And still be doing, never done;
As if religion were intended
For nothing else than to be mended.

GOD CHOSE A STAR

Anonymous

There is mystery in the rose bud and beauty in the blue of sleeping mountains; but there is mystery and beauty and illimitable majesty in the Milky Way.

I do not wonder that God chose a star
To be the sign
For heralding the advent of our Lord;
The still, white shine
Of any star holds something in its heart
Of the Divine.

He chose a star with its clean silver fire,
Its brilliancy,
Its exaltation, and its steadfastness—
Its purity:
The one sign that the shepherds and the kings
Alike, could see.

GOD REST YE, MERRY GENTLEMEN
Dinah Maria Mulock Craik

Mrs. Craik will be remembered for her novel John Halifax, Gentleman, and for her immortal child's story, The Little Lame Prince.

God rest ye, merry gentlemen; let nothing you dismay,
For Jesus Christ, our Saviour, was born on Christmas-day.
The dawn rose red o'er Bethlehem, the stars shone through the gray,
When Jesus Christ, our Saviour, was born on Christmas-day.

God rest ye, little children; let nothing you affright,
For Jesus Christ, your Saviour, was born this happy night;
Along the hills of Galilee the white flocks sleeping lay,
When Christ, the child of Nazareth, was born on Christmas-day.

God rest ye, all good Christians; upon this blessed morn
The Lord of all good Christians was of a woman born:
Now all your sorrows He doth heal, your sins He takes away;
For Jesus Christ, our Saviour, was born on Christmas-day.

GUIDE ME, O THOU GREAT JEHOVAH

William Williams

1717-1791

William Williams is often called the "sweet singer of Wales." This poem was originally a Welsh hymn but was translated into English and later revised in English by the author.

Williams, though he originally studied medicine, came under the influence of the great Whitfield as he heard him preach from a grave-stone pulpit outside the door of the established church. So great was the effect upon young Williams that he gave up medicine for the ministry.

Guide me, O thou great Jehovah,
  Pilgrim through this barren land;
I am weak, but thou art mighty;
  Hold me with thy powerful hand;
    Bread of heaven,
  Feed me till I want no more.

Open thou the crystal fountain
  Whence the healing streams do flow;
Let the fiery, cloudy pillar
  Lead me all my journey through;
    Strong Deliverer,
  Be thou still my Strength and Shield.

THOU ART GOD
The Bible

It is from the Psalms that the Shepherd leads his flock in green pastures beside still waters; here we learn to walk through the valley of the shadow without fear. Of the one hundred and fifty New Testament references to Old Testament writings, one hundred and sixteen are from the Psalms; from out all philosophy there comes no deeper light than this from the Ninetieth Psalm: From everlasting to everlasting, Thou art God.

> Lord, thou hast been our dwelling place
> > In all generations.
>
> Before the mountains were brought forth,
> Or ever thou hadst formed the earth and the world,
> Even from everlasting to everlasting
> > Thou art God.

INDEX

	PAGE
A Forest Hymn—*William Cullen Bryant*	46
A Page from America's Psalter—*Willard Wattles*	54
A Prayer—*Edwin Markham*	108
A Song of Living—*William Stanley Braithwaite*	137
A Star—*Anonymous*	33
A Well-Bred Man—*William Cowper*	16
A Wish—*Samuel Rogers*	34
Abide With Me—*Henry Francis Lyte*	67
Addison, Joseph—An Ode	14
Immortality	30
Aldrich, Thomas Bailey—Identity	118
Alexander, Cecil Frances—The Burial of Moses	18
Along the Road—*Robert Browning Hamilton*	101
An Ode—*Joseph Addison*	14
An Old Woman of the Road—*Padraic Colum*	112
Anonymous—A Star	33
God Chose a Star	146
Horizon	13
Immanence	87
Lord, Take Away Pain	72
Stricken	98
The Anvil	72
The High Road	20
Victory	53
Why Should We Mourn?	83
Apparitions—*Thomas Curtis Clark*	90
Arnold, Matthew—The Last Word	136
Art Thou Weary?—*John Mason Neale*	139
As I Grow Old—*Douglas Malloch*	51
At Jerusalem—*Edna Dean Proctor*	92
Aureole—*Helene Magaret*	125

INDEX

	PAGE
Babcock, Maltbie D.—Our Daily Bread	79
Barabbas—*William E. Brooks*	130
Barbauld, Anna Letitia—Come	132
Baring-Gould, Sabine—Onward Christian Soldiers	36
Bates, David—Speak Gently	136
Benson, Louis FitzGerald—O Love That Lights the Evening Sky	96
Beyond the Horizon—*Robert Freeman*	105
Bible, The—Charity	44
Thou Art God	148
Wisdom	28
Wisdom	131
Black Sheep—*Richard Burton*	56
Bloede, Gertrude—Tomorrows and Tomorrows	28
Bonar, Horatius—I Heard the Voice of Jesus Say	22
Boundaries—*Catherine Cate Coblentz*	49
Bourdillon, Francis William—Upon the Valley's Lap	50
Where Runs the River	78
Braithwaite, William Stanley—A Song of Living	137
Brontë, Emily—The Old Stoic	102
Brooks, William E.—Barabbas	130
Brown, Phoebe—I Love to Steal Awhile Away	80
Browning, Elizabeth Barrett—The Cry of the Children	35
To Sleep	17
Browning, Robert—Guidance	94
Bryant, William Cullen—A Forest Hymn	46
The Good Fight	83
Burns, Robert—On Seeing a Wounded Hare	19
The Cotter's Saturday Night	120
Burton, Richard—Black Sheep	56
Mary Magdalen	62
Butler, Samuel—Hudibras	145
By Night—*Philip Jerome Cleveland*	32
Bynner, Witter—The Poet	71
Byrd, William—My Minde to Me a Kingdom Is	57

INDEX

	PAGE
Byrne, Donn—To the World's Edge	64
Campus—*Margaret Sangster*	132
Channing, William Henry—My Symphony	24
Chapman, Ethelyn Bryant—The Crisis	141
Charity—*The Bible*	44
Christ of the Andes—*Florence Earle Coates*	128
Circumstance—*Alfred Tennyson*	92
Clark, Thomas Curtis—Apparitions	90
Clephane, Elizabeth C.—The Ninety and Nine	77
Cleveland, Philip Jerome—By Night	32
Clough, Arthur Hugh—With Whom Is No Variableness	93
Coates, Florence Earle—Christ of the Andes	128
The House of Pain	15
Coblentz, Catherine Cate—Boundaries	49
Coleridge, Samuel Taylor—He Prayeth Best	129
Colum, Padraic—An Old Woman of the Road	112
Come—*Anna Letitia Barbauld*	132
Conscience—*Nathaniel Hawthorne*	114
Conscience—*William Shakspere*	64
Courage to Live—*Grace Noll Crowell*	89
Cowper, William—A Well-Bred Man	16
Providence	126
The Pledge of Cheerfulness	38
Craik, Dinah Maria Mulock—God Rest Ye, Merry Gentlemen	146
Crosby, Fanny—Saved by Grace	63
Cross, Allen Eastman—The Hidden Years at Nazareth	21
Crowell, Grace Noll—Courage to Live	89
Davies, Mary Caroline—Door-Mats	86
Death—*Emily Dickinson*	113
Dickens, Charles—The Ivy Green	65
Dickinson, Emily—Death	113
Revery	13
The Chariot	103
Divina Commedia—*Henry W. Longfellow*	104

INDEX

	PAGE
Doane, George Washington—Evening Hymn	114
Door-Mats—*Mary Caroline Davies*	86
Doudney, Sarah—The Water Mill	25
Eaton, Virginia—My Neighbor	73
Eliot, George—Oh, May I Join the Choir Invisible	29
Epigram—*Sir William Watson*	85
Evening Hymn—*George Washington Doane*	114
Faber, Frederick William—The Heart of the Eternal	27
Faith and Hope—*Sir Robert Grant*	119
Farewell Address at Springfield—*Abraham Lincoln*	23
Farmers—*William Alexander Percy*	59
Fifer, H. N.—He Lived a Life	97
For One Who Died—*Jessica Powers*	70
Foss, Sam Walter—The True Bible	79
Frank, Florence Kiper—The Jew to Jesus	90
The Jewish Conscript	104
Freeman, Robert—Beyond the Horizon	105
Garrison, Theodosia—The Days	87
The Tears of Mary	116
Stains	74
Gilder, Jeanette—My Creed	37
God Chose a Star—*Anonymous*	146
God Makes a Path—*Roger Williams*	143
God of Our Life Through All the Circling Years—*Hugh T. Kerr*	107
God Rest Ye, Merry Gentlemen—*Dinah Maria Mulock Craik*	146
Gone!—*Ethel Runyon Knott*	27
Good in Everything—*William Shakspere*	81
Grant, Sir Robert—Faith and Hope	119
Guidance—*Robert Browning*	94
Guide Me, O Thou Great Jehovah—*William Williams*	147
Hamilton, Robert Browning—Along the Road	101
Hawthorne, Nathaniel—Conscience	114
He Lived a Life—*H. N. Fifer*	97
He Prayeth Best—*Samuel Taylor Coleridge*	129

INDEX

                                                                                          PAGE

Heber, Reginald—Holy, Holy, Holy!	40
Henley, William Ernest—The Ways of Death	140
Holmes, John A.—Joshua Peabody	61
Holmes, Oliver Wendell—The Old Amati	142
Holy, Holy, Holy!—*Reginald Heber*	40
Hopper, Edward—Jesus, Saviour, Pilot Me	60
Horace	106
Horizon—*Anonymous*	13
Hudibras—*Samuel Butler*	145
Hush, My Dear, Lie Still and Slumber—*Isaac Watts*	100
I Heard the Voice of Jesus Say—*Horatius Bonar*	22
I Love to Steal Awhile Away—*Phoebe Brown*	80
Identity—*Thomas Bailey Aldrich*	118
Immanence—*Anonymous*	87
Immortality—*Joseph Addison*	30
In the Garden of the Lord—*Helen Keller*	106
Indifference—*G. A. Studdert-Kennedy*	82
Ingersoll, Robert G.—The Rustle of a Wing	86
Jesus, Saviour, Pilot Me—*Edward Hopper*	60
Johnson, Josephine—There Is a Tide	41
Johnson, Samuel—Life	43
Joshua Peabody—*John A. Holmes*	61
Joy, Shipmate, Joy—*Walt Whitman*	101
Keller, Helen—In the Garden of the Lord	106
Kennedy, G. A. Studdert—Indifference	82
Kerr, Hugh T.—God of Our Life Through All the Circling Years	107
Kinship—*Angela Morgan*	115
Kirk, Richard R.—We Visit My Estate	75
Knott, Ethel Runyon—Gone!	27
Landor, Walter Savage—No Word of Fear	55
Lee, Agnes—The Christ-Child	43
"Let It Be Forgotten"—*Sara Teasdale*	113
Liddell, George T.—The Christ of Common Folks	55
Life—*Samuel Johnson*	43

INDEX

	PAGE
Life—*Sarojina Nayadu*	115
Lincoln, Abraham—Farewell Address at Springfield	23
Lindsey, Theresa—The Man, Christ	134
Log, Naval Academy—'Tain't	58
Longfellow, Henry—Divina Commedia	104
Stay, Stay at Home, My Heart, and Rest	127
The Bridge	38
Lord, Take Away Pain—*Anonymous*	72
Lyte, Henry Francis—Abide With Me	67
MacDonald, George—When God Thought of You	54
Magaret, Helene—Aureole	125
Malloch, Douglas—As I Grow Old	51
We Call This Life	95
Markham, Edwin—A Prayer	108
Mary at the Cross—*Clyde McGee*	94
Mary Magdalen—*Richard Burton*	62
Matheson, George—O Love That Wilt Not Let Me Go	109
McGee, Clyde—Mary at the Cross	94
Mifflin, Lloyd—The Harvest Waits	66
Miller, Joaquin—The Mothers of Men	133
Mitchell, Silas Weir—Vesperal	68
Morgan, Angela—Kinship	115
My Creed—*Jeanette Gilder*	37
My Faith Looks Up to Thee—*Ray Palmer*	83
"My Heart Leaps Up"—*William Wordsworth*	85
My Minde to Me a Kingdom Is—*William Byrd*	57
My Neighbor—*Virginia Eaton*	73
My Own Song—*Harriet Prescott Spofford*	135
My Symphony—*William Henry Channing*	24
Nayadu, Sarojina—Life	115
Neale, John Mason—Art Thou Weary	139
No Word of Fear—*Walter Savage Landor*	55
O God, Our Help in Ages Past—*Isaac Watts*	84
O Love That Lights the Evening Sky—*Louis FitzGerald Benson*	96

INDEX

	PAGE
O Love That Wilt Not Let Me Go—*George Matheson*	109
O Yet We Trust—*Alfred Tennyson*	81
Oh, May I Join the Choir Invisible—*George Eliot*	29
Old Teacher—*Gerald Raferty*	47
On Seeing a Wounded Hare—*Robert Burns*	19
Onward Christian Soldiers—*Sabine Baring-Gould*	36
Our Daily Bread—*Maltbie D. Babcock*	79
Out to Old Aunt Mary's—*James Whitcomb Riley*	31
Palmer, Ray—My Faith Looks Up to Thee	83
Patmore, Coventry—The Toys	110
Peace—*Clinton Scollard*	107
Percy, William Alexander—Farmers	59
Phillips, Gertie Stewart—Prayer	75
Phillips, Rose Myra—Wanderers	16
Pope, Alexander—The Quiet Life	91
The Universal Prayer (Stanza)	102
Powers, Jessica—For One Who Died	70
Prayer—*Gertie Stewart Phillips*	75
Proctor, Adelaide—The Lost Chord	52
Proctor, Edna Dean—At Jerusalem	92
Providence—*William Cowper*	126
Raferty, Gerald—Old Teacher	47
Revery—*Emily Dickinson*	13
Riley, James Whitcomb—Out to Old Aunt Mary's	31
Rocked in the Cradle of the Deep—*Emma Willard*	42
Rogers, Robert Cameron—The Rosary	47
Rogers, Samuel—A Wish	34
Sangster, Margaret—Campus	132
Saved by Grace—*Fanny Crosby*	63
Saxe, John Godfrey—The Old Man's Motto	144
Scollard, Clinton—Peace	107
Shaw, Frances—Who Loves the Rain	127
Snowbound, From—*John Greenleaf Whittier*	48
Sonnet 73, From—*William Shakspere*	50

INDEX

	PAGE
Shakspere, William—Conscience	64
From Sonnet 73	50
Good in Everything	81
The Primrose Path	98
Silence—*Charles Hanson Towne*	70
So Many—*Frank L. Stanton*	45
Speak Gently—*David Bates*	136
Spofford, Harriet Prescott—My Own Song	135
Stains—*Theodosia Garrison*	74
Stanton, Frank L.—So Many	45
Starbuck, Victor—The Seekers	69
Stay, Stay at Home, My Heart and Rest—*Henry W. Longfellow*	127
Stevenson, Robert Louis—The Celestial Surgeon	99
Still, Still with Thee—*Harriet Beecher Stowe*	99
Stowe, Harriet Beecher—Still, Still with Thee	99
Stricken—*Anonymous*	98
Tabb, John Bannister—The Difference	125
'Tain't—*Naval Academy Log*	58
Teasdale, Sara—"Let It Be Forgotten"	113
Tennyson, Alfred—Circumstance	92
O Yet We Trust	81
The Anvil—*Anonymous*	72
The Bridge—*Henry W. Longfellow*	38
The Burial of Moses—*Cecil Frances Alexander*	18
The Celestial Surgeon—*Robert Louis Stevenson*	99
The Chariot—*Emily Dickinson*	103
The Christ of Common Folks—*George T. Liddell*	55
The Christ-Child—*Agnes Lee*	43
The Christmas Calf—*Judy Van der Veer*	76
The Cotter's Saturday Night—*Robert Burns*	120
The Crisis—*Ethelyn Bryant Chapman*	141
The Cry of the Children—*Elizabeth Barrett Browning*	35
The Days—*Theodosia Garrison*	87
The Difference—*John Bannister Tabb*	125

INDEX

PAGE

The Good Fight—*William Cullen Bryant* 83
The Harvest Waits—*Lloyd Mifflin* 66
The Heart of the Eternal—*Frederick William Faber* 27
The Hidden Years at Nazareth—*Allen Eastman Cross* 21
The High Road—*Anonymous* 20
The House of Pain—*Florence Earle Coates* 15
The Ivy Green—*Charles Dickens* 65
The Jew to Jesus—*Florence Kiper Frank* 90
The Jewish Conscript—*Florence Kiper Frank* 104
The Last Word—*Matthew Arnold* 136
The Lost Chord—*Adelaide Proctor* 52
The Man, Christ—*Theresa Lindsey* 134
The Mothers of Men—*Joaquin Miller* 133
The Ninety and Nine—*Elizabeth C. Clephane* 77
The Old Amati—*Oliver Wendell Holmes* 142
The Old Man's Motto—*John Godfrey Saxe* 144
The Old Stoic—*Emily Brontë* 102
The Pledge of Cheerfulness—*William Cowper* 138
The Poet—*Witter Bynner* 71
The Primrose Path—*William Shakspere* 98
The Quiet Life—*Alexander Pope* 91
The Rosary—*Robert Cameron Rogers* 47
The Rustle of a Wing—*Robert G. Ingersoll* 86
The Seekers—*Victor Starbuck* 69
The Tears of Mary—*Theodosia Garrison* 116
The Toys—*Coventry Patmore* 110
The True Bible—*Sam Walter Foss* 79
The Universal Prayer—*Alexander Pope* 102
The Water Mill—*Sarah Doudney* 25
The Ways of Death—*William Ernest Henley* 140
There Is a Tide—*Josephine Johnson* 41
Thou Art God—*The Bible* 148
To One Self-Slain—*Charles Hanson Towne* 111
To Sleep—*Elizabeth Barrett Browning* 17

INDEX

	PAGE
To the World's Edge—*Donn Byrne*	64
Tomorrows and Tomorrows—*Gertrude Bloede*	28
Towne, Charles Hanson—Silence	70
To One Self-Slain	111
Upon the Valley's Lap—*Francis William Bourdillon*	50
Van der Veer, Judy—The Christmas Calf	76
Vesperal—*Silas Weir Mitchell*	68
Victory—*Anonymous*	53
Wanderers—*Rose Myra Phillips*	16
Watson, Sir William—Epigram	85
Wattles, Willard—A Page from America's Psalter	54
Watts, Isaac—Hush, My Dear, Lie Still and Slumber	100
O God, Our Help in Ages Past	84
We Call This Life—*Douglas Malloch*	95
We Visit My Estate—*Richard R. Kirk*	75
When God Thought of You—*George MacDonald*	54
Where Runs the River—*Francis William Bourdillon*	78
Whitman, Walt—Joy, Shipmate, Joy	101
Whittier, John Greenleaf—From Snowbound	48
Who Loves the Rain—*Frances Shaw*	127
Why Should We Mourn—*Anonymous*	83
Willard, Emma—Rocked in the Cradle of the Deep	42
Williams, Roger—God Makes a Path	143
Williams, William—Guide Me, O Thou Great Jehovah	147
Wisdom—*The Bible*	28
Wisdom—*The Bible*	131
With Whom Is No Variableness—*Arthur Hugh Clough*	93
Wordsworth, William—My Heart Leaps Up	85